THE VIETNAMESE MARKET COOKBOOK

◨ SQUARE PEG

The VIETNAMESE *Market* COOKBOOK

Van Tran and Anh Vu

Photography by Yuki Sugiura

Published by Square Peg 2013

10 9 8 7 6 5 4

Copyright © Van Tran and Anh Vu 2013
Food and travel photography by Yuki Sugiura

First published in Great Britain in 2013 by
Square Peg
Random House, 20 Vauxhall Bridge Road,
London SW1V 2SA
www.vintage-books.co.uk

Addresses for companies within The Random House Group Limited can be found at:
www.randomhouse.co.uk/offices.htm
The Random House Group Limited Reg. No. 954009

A CIP catalogue record for this book is available from the British Library

ISBN 9780224095617

Penguin Random House is committed to a sustainable future for our business,
our readers and our planet. This book is made From Forest Stewardship
Council® certified paper.

Typeset and designed by Anna Crone at www.siulendesign.com
Production by Anna Cowling
Food styling by Valerie Berry
Prop styling by Cynthia Inions

Printed and bound in China by C&C Offset Printing Co. , Ltd
To reflect the mood of Vietnam – the slow pace, the craftsmanship, and the resourcefulness –
most of the photographs in this book were shot on conventional negative film.

To our Mothers,
for beginning

To our Banhmily,
for continuing

CONTENTS

phát triển
đồng cỏ
chăn nuôi

nuôi
nhiều
gà

We were born in Vietnam, a land of bustlingly vibrant food markets. They come to life at dawn, with the clattering of footsteps, straw baskets full of local vegetables and seasonal herbs, barrows weighted down with meat, sacks of freshly baked baguettes, buckets with fish swimming inside, coops with chickens, bamboo presses with fresh tofu, hampers full of speciality mushrooms and spices, and food stalls everywhere. The markets are in the back alleys of Hanoi, in the shadow of high-rises in Saigon, in the misty valleys of Sapa, and on floating boats in the red waters of the Mekong Delta. Cooking, commerce and community make up the rhythm of daily life in Vietnam, and the starting point is a morning visit to the market...

Introduction

Five Fundamental Flavours

In Vietnamese cuisine, the ideal food balances the five flavours of sweet, sour, spicy, bitter and salty. Accordingly, we have arranged the recipes in this book into five chapters, each devoted to one of the five flavours, to help you intuitively understand the principles of Vietnamese cooking. Try to imagine the taste of the dish on the tip of your tongue and then let your palate guide you as you cook.

Each chapter is then divided into three sections. In Vietnam we distinguish between three kinds of eating: *an com, an qua* and *an choi. An* means to eat, but it prefixes many other Vietnamese words, which just goes to show how food is at the heart of our culture.

Everyday cooking we call *An Com*, which literally means to eat rice. This is the classic Vietnamese staple, eaten twice daily. In family meals rice forms the foundation of a holy trinity of (1) savoury meat or fish; (2) a vegetable stir-fry; and (3) an accompanying soup. But today, with our busy lifestyles, we are unlikely to cook all these elements for a simple midweek dinner. Instead, you can mix and match these recipes to make healthy everyday meals.

Festive cooking we call *An Qua. Qua* means a gift. Often in Vietnam it's the amazing combination of flavours in a bowl of noodle soup. Festive cooking can be elaborate, so it's for weekends and celebrations, or simply for when you want to treat yourself.

Social cooking is *An Choi. Choi* means play. This is eating for enjoyment's sake, such as a snack from a specialist one-dish street-food vendor. Here we have included recipes for starters, snacks, drinks and sweet treats. These recipes are perfect for shared plates, party canapés or whenever you fancy bold flavours.

Cooking the Vietnamese Way

An important part of cooking Vietnamese food is learning to develop your own palate – by touching the ingredients, smelling the marinated food, tasting the cooked food, and having the confidence to adjust as you see fit. Every family in Vietnam has a distinct way of cooking, a personal take on what is otherwise a rather orthodox repertoire of dishes. For instance, caramelised braised pork in the north is saltier and saucier than its southern counterpart, which is sweeter and uses coconut milk.

With Vietnam's long history as a sea-facing country with foreign settlers, it's no surprise that our food is a fusion of international influences. Take two of the world's greatest culinary traditions, French and Chinese, throw in a basketful of tropical flavours and fresh herbs, add a dash of Japanese sensitivity and you have the basis of many of the recipes in Vietnam. Consequently, Vietnamese cooking lends itself to adaptation.

Food markets are ubiquitous in Vietnam. It's here that trading and farming, metropolitan and village life come together as growers and consumers interact. Vietnamese cooking is based on market-fresh ingredients. We look for whatever is in season, harvested that day. We understand that while vegetables might not be perfectly uniform and identically packaged, they must be bursting with flavour. Our cooking is naturally intuitive and versatile. We cook by what the season brings and the market offers, not the vagaries of celebrity chefs!

Craft Banhmi Experience
Step 1: What meal would you like
Bánh mì £5
Toasted demi baguette
Bún £6
Rice vermicelli salad
Step 2: What filling would you like

Imperial BBQ Pork
with lemongrass & caramel

Fish Q

Pho
Sophy
www.phosophy.co.uk

Pho Noodle Soup
Fresh handmade rice noodles
in 72 hours beef broth

BÚN £6
Noodle salad with
rice vermicelli

CƠM £6
Rice box with sushi
rice

All of our meals are served with

IMPERIAL
Grilled pork,
and lemongrass

FISH Q
Grilled catfish
turmeric, with

CHA CHA C
Grilled chicken
in coconut mil

TEMPLE
slow-simmered
and sour pineap

PRAWN   SEABASS

Our Story
– Van Tran

Anh and I were born eleven months apart in the same city, Hanoi. The capital was previously known as Ke Cho, which translates as marketplace.

My earliest memory is of holding my mother's hand down a street lined with purple blossoming *bang lang* trees on our way to the local market. The daily trip to the market was a ritual: at the entrance fruit stands were overflowing with lychees and papayas; further on, butchers' stalls each specialised in one type of meat. My mother would select a cut of meat and plan the day's menu around it. She would visit the dry goods stalls for spices by weight and noodles in all shapes and sizes. To complete the meal she would pick a vegetable for soup, another for a stir-fry, and a handful of fresh herbs. These daily trips to the market gave us joy at the table. They instilled in me not only a love of food but also an appreciation of how it brings people together and spreads warmth.

Markets were so ingrained in our consciousness, that when Anh and I visited Broadway Market in London's East End a year after we moved to the UK, we instantly recognised a missing piece of our lives. There's Matthew, who raises his cows and pigs on organic land in Suffolk. Then there's Jony, who sells sourdough bread so tasty we have midweek cravings. And there's Tamami, who single-handedly bakes wholesome cakes in her small kitchen oven while her children sleep. We identified with these people, their market-fresh way of eating and sense of community. Echoing our childhood rituals, Saturday morning visits to Broadway Market became a routine. Then, as the kitchen gods would have it, we became stallholders at Broadway Market – Banhmi11 was born in the summer of 2009. We started out with recipes passed down from Anh's mother, who used to have a *banh mi* stall in Hanoi. For the first year, we made pâté, roast pork and pickles in our tiny home kitchen and brought everything to the stall on the back of our bicycles. What follows is what happens after love at first bite.

CHAPTER ONE

SWEETNESS

— AND —

Happiness

Sweetness is perhaps the most obviously pleasing of the five flavours. Its familiarity stretches back to childhood treats, like the colourful birthday cakes that marked our annual milestones.

By sweetness we don't just mean the puddings and treats that would classify as a 'sweet' on a Western menu. We mean the subtle notes that underpin certain dishes, be they savoury or sweet. This chapter includes some obviously sweet ingredients like seductive soft fruits. But it also includes more unlikely candidates: vegetables such as pumpkin and marrow, which add a sweet note to soup within minutes; and meat and seafood, which, when cooked the right way, release a deep and succulent sweetness.

The savoury recipes in this chapter all have sweet qualities, for example the pork belly which is steeped in caramelised sugar then slowly simmered to release a wonderfully honeyed flavour.

In this chapter we include a classic Vietnamese noodle soup called *pho*. For us, *pho* is all about sweetness, despite being a main course. In the same way Western soups use stock, *pho* is based on a broth made from slowly boiled bones. This slow-cooked broth releases a delightful sweetness which is intrinsic to the dish.

Anh and I still believe the most authentic *pho* noodle soup is only found in the Old Quarter of Hanoi. The Hanoian palate prefers a gentle sweetness, not the saccharine, MSG-laden offerings of ersatz versions. Hanoi's *pho* is simple: a clear stock, tender meat, a fine sprinkling of fresh herbs, a couple of slices of fresh chilli, a wedge of lime, and no cluttering with beansprouts.

The soul of this *pho* is the broth – the fragrance is irresistible: cinnamon, cardamom, star anise, coriander seeds and ginger. The sweetness of *pho* is deep: it doesn't hit the tip of your tongue, but leaves a satisfying kick at the back of your throat.

The first time I had *pho* in Vietnam as a grown-up was on my first return visit after moving away, and it was then that I understood why my mother had always gone to the effort of making this dish during the years we lived outside Vietnam.

We sat on plastic stools in the heat of Hanoi in July and watched as steaming ladles of broth were poured into large white bowls that gleamed in the early morning sun. Here in Vietnam, street food is simply home cooking that has sprawled out onto the street. People open up their shop-front living rooms, put out more chairs and tables on the pavement and serve from a stall set up by the entrance.

As we sipped the *pho*, my mother commented on how soft the fresh, hand-made noodles were. I had never seen her so content, so at home. For the first time, I saw her as a friend, as a person with her own life story, secrets and dreams. And for the first time I understood the power of food to spark memories and make you feel at home. I saw how the cuisine carries the culture. Never again would I question why my mother went to such lengths to replicate Hanoian recipes abroad. Through her cooking she rooted us in family tradition.

That afternoon, my mother went to the hairdresser and got her hair done in the exact same style she wore in those old black and white photos of her hanging on the wall at home. Suddenly she seemed as youthful as me, in her twenties with everything ahead of her. The sweetness of that day still lingers.

Everyday Cooking
(An Com)

The Vietnamese don't eat their meals in the sequential order of starter, main course and dessert. At mealtimes the dishes are laid out together and everyone is called to the table. However simple the meal, the trinity of a protein main course, a vegetable side and a soup is honoured. The nurturer of the family, whether it be the mother or the eldest son, is given the important task of serving everyone rice, and typically two bowls is mandatory. Fruits and tea are served afterwards. This traditional Vietnamese format is designed for communal dining. But you can pick out any dish you fancy from the following recipes and enjoy it alone. Or pick any selection to enjoy together with friends and family.

Prawn and Marrow Soup

Soup forms an indispensable part of the Vietnamese meal. It's served together with the main course, usually poured over rice. We make easy, everyday soups from the simplest of ingredients: we boil a vegetable from the fridge, add a pinch of sea salt, muddle in a tomato or a few slices of ginger, and *voilà*. The natural sweetness of many vegetables makes them the mainstay of a comforting soup. Marrow is one of our favourite winter squash, and one of the most dependable vegetables. We use it a chunk at a time, like a good piece of farmhouse Cheddar, and the marrow lasts us a whole week. In this recipe, you can equally well use courgettes.

Serves 2

200g fresh prawns, peeled
200g chunk of marrow
1 tbsp vegetable oil
½ tsp crushed garlic
750ml hot water
1 tsp gia vi (or a mix of
   2 parts sugar, 1 part
   sea salt, 1 part ground
   black pepper, 1 part
   garlic powder)
2 tbsp fish sauce
1 tbsp chopped spring
   onion

Marinade:
1 tsp freshly ground black
   pepper
1 tbsp fish sauce
½ tsp chopped garlic

Chop the prawns coarsely.

Combine all the marinade ingredients and pour over the prawns. Cover and leave to marinate for a couple of minutes while you prepare the marrow.

Peel the marrow, cut in half lengthways and remove any seeds. Then use a vegetable peeler to slice the marrow into thin slices of about 1mm.

In a heavy-bottomed pan, heat the oil then stir in the garlic until the oil is fragrant. Pour in the marinated prawns and stir quickly until they turn pink.

Pour in the hot water and leave to boil, skimming off any foam that builds up.

Season with the gia vi and the fish sauce, and add the marrow slices. Cook for about 5 minutes until soft.

Take off the heat and sprinkle with the chopped spring onion before serving.

Note: if you want the broth to be extra sweet then buy unpeeled prawns to peel yourself. Cook the shells separately in the 750ml of water for 5–10 minutes. Remove the shells before adding the water to the sautéed prawns.

Asparagus and Crabmeat Soup

We are big fans of asparagus. In late spring, when asparagus is plentiful at the market, we pick up a couple of bunches every week. It is so versatile – we boil it with a dash of ginger, or make a stir-fry (see p.164), or pan-fry it lightly with a smidgen of butter, a dash of lemon juice and a sprinkling of sesame.

Asparagus and crabmeat scream luxurious cooking, but the truth is you need only use a modest amount of each to create a big splash.

Serves 4

1.5l chicken stock (see
  chicken broth recipe on
  p.193 or use ready-made)
1 tbsp vegetable oil
1 tbsp chopped shallot
100g white crabmeat
1 tsp fish sauce
2 tbsp cornflour
4 tbsp cold water
1 bunch asparagus
50g fresh shiitake
  mushrooms (or 20g dried)
Freshly ground black
  pepper, to taste
2 tbsp chopped fresh
  coriander, to serve

In a large pan, bring the chicken stock to the boil.

In a separate, heavy-bottomed pan, heat the oil then stir in the chopped shallot, stirring quickly until the oil is fragrant. Add the crabmeat and flash-fry for a couple of minutes, before seasoning with the fish sauce.

In a bowl, dissolve the cornflour in the cold water.

Chop the asparagus into 1cm rounds.

Slice the shiitake mushrooms thinly. (If using dried shiitake, soak them in hot water for about 15 minutes, drain and then pat dry with a paper towel before slicing.)

Once the chicken stock is boiling, add the seasoned crabmeat, along with the asparagus and shiitake mushrooms. Bring to the boil again and stir in the cornflour mixture. Stir for a couple of minutes as the soup thickens and then take off the heat.

Grind some fresh pepper over the soup and sprinkle the chopped coriander in the bowls before serving.

Grind over some more pepper at the table before eating.

Artichoke and Pork Ribs Soup

When a vegetable as aristocratic as the artichoke is combined with something as common as pork ribs, the resulting sweetness is wonderfully ethereal.

Serves 2

300g small pork loin ribs
4–6 artichoke hearts
1 tsp gia vi (or a mix of
   2 parts sugar, 1 part
   sea salt, 1 part ground
   black pepper, 1 part
   garlic powder)
2 tsp fish sauce
1 tsp chopped spring onion
1 tsp chopped fresh
   coriander

Bring a large pan of water to the boil and add the pork ribs. Boil for a couple of minutes only, then pour the water out and discard the first broth. (This is to cleanse the ribs, so don't cook for too long as they will lose their sweetness.)

Put the ribs back into the pan. Add enough water to come about 5cm above the ribs and bring to the boil again.

Add the artichokes and cook until soft. Stir in the gia vi along with the fish sauce.

Sprinkle with the chopped spring onion and coriander and serve hot.

Note: you can ask the butcher to chop the ribs into small 3cm chunks.

Chicken, Cauliflower and Spring Onion Soup

Often when we have a good chicken stock to hand we like to make a *pho* noodle soup (see p.42). On grey autumn evenings, however, we go for a really plain, clear soup. It is both simple and soothing.

Serves 4

1.5l chicken stock (see
   chicken broth recipe on
   p.193 or use ready-made)
½ cauliflower
1 tsp gia vi (or a mix of
   2 parts sugar, 1 part
   sea salt, 1 part ground
   black pepper, 1 part
   garlic powder)
2 tsp fish sauce
1 tsp chopped spring onion
1 tsp chopped fresh
   coriander

In a large pan, bring the chicken stock to the boil.

Cut the cauliflower into florets, add to the broth and cook until soft.

Season to taste with the gia vi and fish sauce.

Sprinkle the chopped spring onion and coriander over the broth and serve hot.

Pumpkin Braised with Coconut

Throughout winter we have pumpkins in our vegetable box in the kitchen. We often slice them thinly then stir-fry with lots of crushed garlic. But after they've been sitting in the vegetable box for some time their flesh begins to dry out, so we discovered you could remedy that by cutting them into thick chunks and cooking them like a curry with coconut milk. Coconut milk injects the pumpkin with moisture and brings the flavours back to life.

Serves 2

250g pumpkin, peeled
  and deseeded
1 tbsp vegetable oil
½ tbsp chopped shallot
2 tbsp soy sauce
100ml coconut milk
1 tbsp chopped spring
  onion
1 tbsp chopped fresh
  coriander

Cut the pumpkin into chunks.

In a heavy-bottomed pan, heat the oil and toss in the shallot. Stir in the pumpkin and season with the soy sauce, then add just enough water to cover the pumpkin.

Simmer over a medium heat until the pumpkin is soft, which should take about 15 minutes.

Pour in the coconut milk and simmer for another 15 minutes.

Sprinkle the chopped spring onion and coriander on top.

Caramelised Braised Pork Belly

My father was born in the countryside and although he's now a scientist with two doctorates, he has retained a penchant for simple, country comfort food. He loves leftover rice fried with greens, or sticky rice with caramelised pork. As my father completed his studies in Germany, I didn't meet him until I was three, but I inherited from him a love of caramelised pork. It's a staple dish at our kitchen table, especially in the winter months. In this recipe, the slow simmering of the pork makes it deliciously sweet and tender.

Serves 4

300g slab pork belly
2 slices fresh ginger
200ml coconut milk

Marinade:
1 tbsp gia vi (or a mix of
  2 parts sugar, 1 part
  sea salt, 1 part ground
  black pepper, 1 part
  garlic powder)
2 tbsp fish sauce
1 tsp chopped shallot

Caramel sauce:
4 tsp sugar
200ml hot water

Bring water to a boil in a large pan or stockpot and throw in the ginger. Add the pork (don't cut into chunks at this stage or it will cook too quickly and lose its sweetness) and cook for about 3–4 minutes over a high heat to blanch the meat.

In a bowl, mix together the marinade ingredients. Slice the pork belly into 2cm chunks, rub in the marinade, then cover and leave for at least 15 minutes.

To caramelise the sugar, pour the sugar into a heavy-bottomed braising pan or cast-iron casserole. Place over a medium heat, without stirring, for 2–3 minutes, then reduce the heat and stir constantly until no grains of sugar are visible. This should take about 2–3 minutes. The sugar will then begin to melt and become golden in colour. Pay attention to the colour of the caramel underneath the bubbles. Add the hot water and cook until it boils. Don't worry if the sugar hardens upon contact with the water; it will re-melt as it cooks, forming a sauce.

Add the marinated pork to the braising pan, making sure all the meat gets coated with the caramel sauce.

Pour in the coconut milk and stir, then leave it for another minute. Taste and add more fish sauce or sugar if necessary, depending on whether it's a little too sweet or salty.

Reduce the heat and leave the meat to simmer for about 30 minutes, until the braising liquid has reduced and thickened.

This is best served with white rice and a sour salad like the Red Cabbage and Beansprout Salad on p.86, which cuts through its sweetness.

Egg-glazed Aubergine Fritters

On Saturday nights, after spending the whole day selling street food on Broadway Market, we are usually so tired and half-full from grazing on food we've swapped with the other traders, that we always cook something simple like these aubergine fritters. We thought of tempura batter, which works for any vegetable, from cauliflower to courgette slices, then we made our batter even more simple by literally just cracking an egg, whisking with a fork and dipping the thinly sliced aubergine into it. We munch on them as they come out of the pan, savouring the rich sweetness of the egg and the softness of the aubergine.

Serves 2

1 medium-sized aubergine
1 egg
1 tsp fish sauce
1 tbsp vegetable oil

Cut the aubergine in half and then cut each half into thin slices, a few millimetres thick.

Whisk the egg and season with the fish sauce.

Heat the oil in a frying pan.

Dip the aubergine slices, one at a time, in the egg liquid and then immediately add to the pan and fry until golden. Carefully remove to a plate lined with a paper towel to drain. Serve warm.

Beef au Vin *(Bo Sot Vang)*

Beef was not part of the Vietnamese diet until the French arrived in the late 19th century and started to import it. Although there were buffalos in Vietnam, they were work animals only and designated as holy.

Like most French dishes that came to Vietnam, this recipe changed en route, and the beef stew is now spiced with strong flavours like cinnamon and star anise.

We love this recipe, which we got from friends in New York, because it feels sumptuous yet comforting. When we're feeling weary all we need is to be fed a bowl of warm, sweet and perfectly spiced stew.

Serves 4

1kg diced stewing beef
500g tomatoes
1l water
1 cinnamon stick (20g)
1 star anise
200g carrots

Marinade:
100ml red wine
1 tbsp gia vi (or a mix of 2 parts sugar, 1 part sea salt, 1 part ground black pepper, 1 part garlic powder)
2 tbsp fish sauce
½ tsp cinnamon powder
2 tbsp sugar
50g grated fresh ginger
1 tsp crushed garlic

Place the marinade ingredients in a bowl and mix well. Add the diced beef to the bowl and rub in the marinade with your hands. Cover and leave in the fridge for at least 30 minutes.

Cut each tomato in half and then slice each half into thirds.

Put a heavy-bottomed pan on a medium-high heat. Once it's hot, add the marinated beef and cook, stirring constantly, so the beef does not burn. After 5–10 minutes, lower the heat, add the tomatoes and simmer for another 10 minutes until soft.

Add up to 1 litre boiling water to the pan – enough to just cover the meat – along with the cinnamon stick and star anise. Slow-cook on a low heat for at least 45 minutes. Check on the beef every now and then and add more water if it has reduced too much.

About 15 minutes before serving, cut the carrots into pieces about 1cm thick. Add to the pan and simmer until soft and ready to eat. Fish out the cinnamon stick and star anise before serving.

We tend to eat this stew very simply with a fresh baguette. It is also great with rice or potatoes.

Note: you can make this recipe with oxtail too – just double the stewing time.

Festive Cooking (An Qua)

Festive cooking in Vietnam falls into two categories. The first is the multi-course banquet served at public occasions like weddings, wakes, anniversaries, birthdays and events to honour elders or even ancestors. Traditional dishes like spring rolls are beautifully arranged on platters, and the extended family and neighbours (which in the country means the whole village) are wined and dined. The second type of festive cooking is at more intimate family celebrations like Sundays at the grandparents'.

Slow-cooked broths and sweet marinated meats have a natural place at festive gatherings.

Imperial BBQ Pork

Here we have adapted a traditional Hanoian marinade by adding lemongrass and chilli. This pork is perfect served with vermicelli noodles and a herb salad (see p.38). We also use it in our *banh mi* baguettes (see p.36), and it is the most popular filling at our stall. You can also serve it in a summer roll (see p.171).

Serves 4

1kg pork shoulder,
 off the bone

Marinade:
1 tbsp finely chopped
 shallot
1 tbsp finely chopped
 spring onion
1 tsp crushed garlic
4 tbsp fish sauce
½ tbsp salt
½ tbsp freshly ground
 black pepper
1 tbsp finely chopped
 lemongrass
4 tbsp sugar
¼ tbsp chilli powder
250ml caramel water
 (see p.194)

Slice the pork shoulder thinly, into about 2mm slices. The thinner you slice the meat, the better it will absorb flavours.

In a bowl, combine all the marinade ingredients. Add the pork and mix well, rubbing the marinade in vigorously with your hands. Cover and leave in the fridge for at least an hour before cooking, ideally overnight.

Thread the pork on to skewers and grill for 10–15 minutes, turning frequently.

Note: you could also cook this on a barbecue or in the oven. For the latter, put the skewers on a rack over a foil-lined baking tray so the oil can drip through, then cook in a preheated oven at 180°C/gas 4 for about 25–30 minutes until brown. The traditional Vietnamese way of cooking the pork is on a metal grill 'net' (see photo opposite). You can buy nets in Asian supermarkets. Spread the pork in a layer over the net and put the net on the grill or in a very hot oven. Because the pork is in a single layer it chars on the outside without drying out in the middle.

To slice the meat thinly, you can part-freeze it first (see p.209).

Basic Vietnamese Baguette *(Banh Mi)*

A *banh mi* combines a variety of individual ingredients in a baguette. The filling could include anything from barbecued pork to grilled fish, topped with pickles and fresh herbs to create a culinary delight. Here we give you the 'essential' *banh mi*, pared down to the key ingredients you won't want to do without.

Makes 1

20g country pâté
10g unsalted butter
1 demi-baguette
1 tsp mayonnaise
1 squirt chilli sauce
1 fresh chilli, chopped
3–4 slices cucumber
2–3 sprigs coriander

Preheat the oven to 180°C/gas 4. In a small pan, melt the pâté with the unsalted butter, or put the pâté and butter in a small microwave-safe bowl in the microwave for about 1 minute so it is warm and spreadable.

Split the baguette lengthways – you might need to remove some of the doughy filling inside.

Smear a layer of mayo on the top half of the baguette – just enough to moisten the bread without drenching it – and spread the melted pâté on the bottom half.

Toast in the oven for 3–5 minutes so the inside is warm and the outside is crispy. Take care not to burn the bread.

Remove from the oven, using tongs or chopsticks, and flip open the baguette.

Spread a little chilli sauce on the pâté and scatter some chopped chilli on top.

Arrange slices of cucumber and sprigs of coriander neatly along the baguette.

Close the baguette and use a small knife to push all the ingredients inside.

Imperial BBQ Pork Vietnamese Baguette (Banh Mi)

Each of the ingredients in a *banh mi* is potentially a recipe in itself and at Banhmi11 we make everything from scratch. Luckily, these days you can buy nearly all the ingredients ready to go. If you have a good farmers' market near you, get hold of some proper butter, *pâté de campagne*, and of course a crisp baguette. It's also worth hunting down authentic chilli sauce from an Asian grocer. Perhaps the only thing we would encourage you to spend extra time on is home-made pickle, which adds a mouthwatering sourness and crunch to your *banh mi*.

Makes 1

1 tsp country pâté
½ tsp unsalted butter
1 demi-baguette
1 tsp mayonnaise
Carrot and Daikon Pickle, to taste (see p.196)
80–100g Imperial BBQ Pork (see p.32)
1 squirt chilli sauce, or to taste
1 fresh chilli, chopped
3–4 slices cucumber
2–3 sprigs coriander

Preheat the oven to 180°C/gas 4. In a small pan, melt the pâté with the unsalted butter, or put the pâté and butter in a small microwave-safe bowl in the microwave for about 1 minute so it is warm and spreadable.

Split the baguette lengthways – you might need to remove some of the doughy filling inside.

Smear a layer of mayo on the top half of the baguette – just enough to moisten the bread without drenching it – and spread the melted pâté on the bottom half.

Toast in the oven for 3–5 minutes so the inside is warm and the outside is crispy. Take care not to burn the bread.

Remove from the oven, using tongs or chopsticks, and flip open the baguette.

Add a thin layer of Carrot and Daikon Pickle on the pâté – squeezing out any pickle brine first so the bread stays dry and crisp – then top with the grilled pork.

Spread a little chilli sauce on the meat and scatter some chopped chilli on top.

Arrange slices of cucumber and sprigs of coriander neatly along the baguette.

Close the baguette and use a small knife to push all the ingredients inside.

Imperial BBQ Pork Noodle Salad
(Bun Cha)

Anh's mother is a woman of many talents. Now well into her seventies, she still rides her faithful, old Honda 82 scooter fearlessly round Hanoi's rush hour, carrying Anh on the back through snaking queues of traffic.

She has done a lot of things in her life, and most of them had something to do with food. Anh's first memory is of helping her mum seal bags of roast peanuts to sell. When Anh was very little, her mother retired from teaching and set up a noodle salad or *bun cha* stall, which was the first in a string of stalls. She rented a small space on the pavement near Anh's nursery – a treat for people travelling on the main road out from Hanoi.

Serves 4

1–2 packs rice vermicelli
   noodles
200g Imperial BBQ Pork
   (see p.32)
100g beansprouts
50g Carrot and Daikon
   Pickle (see p.196)
Small bunch of mint,
   chopped
Black pepper, to taste

To serve:
Garlic, Lime and Chilli
   Dipping Sauce (see p.198)

Cook the noodles according to the packet instructions. Then tip the noodles into your bowls – they should fill a quarter or a third of each bowl, depending on your preference.

Arrange the meat on the noodles. Garnish with the beansprouts, pickle and mint.

To serve, make up the Garlic, Lime and Chilli Dipping Sauce on p.198 and drizzle over each bowl. Finish with some black pepper.

Classic Beef Noodle Soup *(Pho Bo)*

A truly authentic beef *pho* takes time to make. We cook ours for over 72 hours! But if you're cooking for the family, you can do everything in a day and you will have amazing *pho* for dinner. The broth, with the added spices, can be prepared in advance and it will keep in the fridge for a couple of days, or it can be frozen and kept for a couple of weeks in the freezer. Apart from the meat preparation, *pho* pretty much cooks itself, which is why it's perfect for big festive gatherings.

Serves 4

400g sirloin steak

Marinade:
1 tbsp grated fresh ginger
1 tbsp fish sauce
1 tsp gia vi (or a mix of
  2 parts sugar, 1 part
  sea salt, 1 part ground
  black pepper, 1 part
  garlic powder)

Broth:
2l beef stock (or home-made
  beef broth, see p.192)
2 garlic cloves
2 star anise
2 cardamoms
1 cinnamon stick (20g)
1 large onion, unpeeled
300g piece fresh ginger,
  unpeeled
2 tbsp gia vi (or a mix of
  2 parts sugar, 1 part
  sea salt, 1 part ground
  black pepper, 1 part
  garlic powder)
2 tbsp fish sauce, plus 2 tsp
  for serving
1 tbsp brown sugar

Slice the sirloin steak very thinly. Combine the marinade ingredients in a bowl and add the steak. Cover and leave to marinate while you prepare the rest of the ingredients.

In a large pan or stockpot, bring the beef stock to the boil and add the garlic cloves, star anise, cardamoms and cinnamon. Simmer on a low heat while you prepare the onion and ginger.

Char the onion and ginger over an open flame on the hob, letting the skin burn for about 15 minutes, using tongs to rotate them occasionally, until they become softer and fragrant. Or grill them for 15 minutes, turning them over halfway. Then remove the charred skin, wash the onion and ginger and add whole to the broth.

Simmer the broth for 30 minutes and then discard the onion, ginger and whole spices.

Add the gia vi, fish sauce and brown sugar. Taste and adjust with more salt or sugar as necessary.

To assemble pho bowls:
1–2 packs dried pho
   noodles
4 tbsp finely chopped spring
   onions
1 bunch coriander, finely
   chopped
Black pepper, to taste

To serve:
4 lime wedges
1–2 fresh chillies, or to taste,
   chopped

To assemble the pho bowls:
Cook the noodles according to the packet instructions. Then tip the noodles into your bowls – they should fill a quarter or a third of each bowl, depending on your preference.

Arrange the meat on the noodles. Garnish with the spring onion and coriander. Add ½ tsp of fish sauce to each bowl and finish with some black pepper.

Bring the broth to a bubbling boil. Plunge the ladle deeply to the bottom of the pot, where the broth is hottest, and ladle into each bowl, distributing it evenly so it cooks the raw meat and warms the other ingredients.

The meat will be cooked but rare so if you prefer your meat better done, then in a separate frying pan add 1 tbsp of oil and, when hot, add 1 tsp of garlic. Cook until fragrant then add the strips of meat and flash-fry before adding it to your bowls.

Serve with wedges of lime and fresh chilli to taste.

Note: when you add the fish sauce, pour a small quantity into a ladle and slowly dip the ladle in the broth in a circular motion until the ladle is fully submerged. This ensures that the pungent fish sauce smell disperses so it doesn't overwhelm the dish.

Classic Chicken Noodle Soup *(Pho Ga)*

My mother told me that in the fifties there was no beef on Mondays and Fridays, and this is why chicken *pho* was invented. Some *pho* fanatics considered it sacrilege while others warmed to the lighter sweetness of chicken *pho* broth. The debate between followers of beef and chicken *pho* still rages. The chicken *pho* camp consider it more sophisticated, with its clear broth, thinly shredded white meat and long strips of spring onion. For the best flavour, use a boiler chicken, which you can often find at halal butchers. Otherwise, buy free-range from the farmers' market. Or do as we do and buy a chicken carcass (from Matthew at Broadway Market) – nobody wants them and they make terrific broths.

Serves 4

2l chicken stock (or home-made broth, see p. 193)
400g shredded cooked chicken

Broth seasoning:
2 garlic cloves
2 star anise
2 cardamoms
1 cinnamon stick (20g)
1 large onion, unpeeled
300g piece fresh ginger, unpeeled
2 tbsp gia vi (or a mix of 2 parts sugar, 1 part sea salt, 1 part ground black pepper, 1 part garlic powder)
2 tbsp fish sauce, plus 2 tsp for serving
1 tbsp brown sugar

In a large pan or stockpot, bring the chicken stock or broth to the boil and add the garlic cloves, star anise, cardamoms and cinnamon. Simmer on a low heat while you prepare the onion and ginger.

Char the onion and ginger over an open flame on the hob, letting the skin burn for about 15 minutes, using tongs to rotate them occasionally, until they become softer and fragrant. Or grill them for 15 minutes, turning them over halfway. Then remove the charred skin, wash the onion and ginger and add whole to the broth.

Simmer the broth for 30 minutes then discard the onion, ginger and whole spices.

Add the gia vi, fish sauce and brown sugar. Taste and adjust with more salt or sugar as necessary.

To assemble pho bowls:
1–2 packs dried pho
noodles
200g finely chopped spring
onions
1 bunch coriander, finely
chopped
Black pepper, to taste

To serve:
4 lime wedges
1–2 fresh chillies, or to taste,
chopped

To assemble the pho bowls:
Cook the noodles according to the packet instructions. Then tip the noodles into your bowls – they should fill a quarter or a third of each bowl, depending on your preference.

Arrange the shredded chicken on the noodles. Garnish with the spring onions and coriander. Add ½ tsp fish sauce to each bowl and finish with some black pepper.

Bring the broth to a bubbling boil. Check the seasoning one last time, adjusting if needed, then ladle the broth into each bowl, distributing it evenly.

Serve with wedges of lime and fresh chilli to taste.

Note: when you add the fish sauce, pour a small quantity into a ladle and slowly dip the ladle in the broth in a circular motion until the ladle is fully submerged. This ensures that the pungent fish sauce smell disperses so it doesn't overwhelm the dish.

Pho Ga (top) & Pho Bo (bottom)

Bun Thang

Stairway to Heaven Noodle Soup
(Bun Thang)

I had my first bowl of *bun thang* in my third grade. Our teacher ran a half-day boarding scheme at her house, where we would receive extra tuition in the morning, eat lunch made by her mother, and then be transported to our formal afternoon classes on cyclos. I remember thinking, I don't want to move on to the next grade.

Bun is a noodle made from rice. *Thang* is understood to come from the word *tang*, meaning soup in Chinese. In Vietnamese, *thang* means stairs so it reminds us of the many steps required to construct this noodle soup. At Banhmi11, we call this the 'stairway to heaven soup'. *Bun thang* is typical of Hanoi cuisine – it uses no spicy flavours like lemongrass or chilli, but still achieves a fantastically complex flavour.

Serves 4

50g dried shiitake mushrooms
2–3 tsp vegetable oil
1 large egg, beaten
100g Vietnamese pork ham (optional)
400g shredded cooked chicken
200g cooked king prawns

Broth:
2l chicken stock (or home-made chicken broth, see p.193)
2 tbsp gia vi (or a mix of 2 parts sugar, 1 part sea salt, 1 part ground black pepper, 1 part garlic powder)
2 tbsp fish sauce, plus 2 tsp for serving
1 tbsp brown sugar
1 tbsp diluted shrimp paste (see p.209)

Soak the dried shiitake in warm water until soft, then drain and let them dry. Chop into small thin strips.

Heat the oil in a wok or frying pan on a medium heat and fry the beaten egg in a very thin omelette. Once cooled a little, remove to a chopping board and slice the egg into long thin strips.

Prepare the pork ham by slicing it into long thin strips.

Bring the chicken stock to the boil in a large pan. Turn the heat down to low then add the gia vi, fish sauce and brown sugar.

Add the diluted shrimp paste (prepared as per p.209).

Taste the broth and adjust with more salt or sugar as necessary.

To assemble bun thang
bowls:
1–2 packs dried rice
vermicelli noodles
4 tbsp finely chopped spring
onions
1 small bunch rau ram or
coriander, finely chopped
Black pepper, to taste

To assemble the bun thang bowls:
Cook the noodles according to the packet instructions and divide between your bowls.

Arrange the shredded chicken and prawns (and the slices of Vietnamese pork ham, if using) on the noodles.

Divide the shiitake mushrooms and fried egg strips between the bowls.

Sprinkle the spring onions and chopped herbs over the meat. Add ½ tsp of fish sauce to each bowl and finish with black pepper.

Bring the broth to a bubbling boil and ladle it into each bowl, distributing it evenly.

Note: another authentic ingredient you can include in this dish is prawn floss. Take 50g dried shrimp and soak in hot water for 20 minutes. Then mince the shrimp in a blender until very flaky. Put a wok on medium heat and add the minced shrimp. Stir continuously with a wooden spoon for 5–10 minutes until dry. Transfer the shrimp to a plate and let it cool before adding to the bowls along with the meat.

Social Cooking
(An Choi)

Eating in Vietnam is almost always a social event. Sometimes it feels as if all social activities there are centred around food! There is shopping at the market; whizzing on scooters to catch the street-food vendors who pitch up for an hour a day with just one type of dish; and sitting in cafés, sipping cups of Vietnamese coffee.

Social food tends to be in smaller and lighter portions, but it usually packs a flavourful punch. There's scope for imagination when it comes to shared plates, snacks and sweets. Nature plays its part here, not only in the scent and colour of ingredients, but also in their presentation. In Vietnam sticky rice is wrapped in earthy lotus leaves, beef is grilled on lemongrass skewers, and fish is folded in fragrant banana leaves. Sticks of sugar cane make delicious substitutes for metal skewers, lending sweetness to recipes like barbecued prawns. For dessert or a teatime snack we usually have fresh fruit, or sometimes a pudding like crème caramel.

Prawn Pops

We cooked these prawn pops at our first-ever supper club. We held our pop-up at F. Cooke, the eel and mash shop on Broadway Market, and the electricity went on the blink every five minutes! For an authentic Vietnamese presentation, mould the pops onto sticks of sugar cane or lemongrass rather than metal skewers.

You can prepare the pops a day in advance and keep in the fridge, then quickly fry them before your guests arrive. They can be served as an appetiser or party finger food, or as a main course with vermicelli noodles and a dipping sauce.

Serves 4

500g tiger prawns, fresh
  or frozen, peeled
3 tsp fish sauce, plus 1 tsp
  for serving
1 tsp freshly ground black
  pepper, plus a pinch
1 tsp sugar
1 tsp crushed garlic
50ml annatto seed oil
  (see p.191) or vegetable oil
Vegetable oil for frying
1 spring onion
15–20 sugar cane sticks for
  assembling pops (optional)

Grind the prawns into a paste in a food processor with 3 tsp of fish sauce, 1 tsp of pepper and the sugar and garlic.

Mix 2 tsp of the annatto seed oil (or vegetable oil) into the paste.

Tip the paste into a bowl. Using a firm hand, stir the paste again in the bowl for a couple of minutes, pressing it against the sides until it is dough-like with a spongy consistency.

Scoop out a spoonful of paste at a time, and flatten it out in the palm of your hand. Then put a sugar cane stick in the middle, and by clenching your hand, wrap the paste around the stick until it looks like a popsicle. Be careful not to make it too big so that the paste can cook easily.

Use the same process with more sticks until you have used up all the paste.

Use a pastry brush to brush some annatto seed oil (or vegetable oil) on the outside of each pop.

Add about 2cm of vegetable oil to a frying pan – just enough to cover and shallow-fry the pops. Put the pan on a medium-low heat and, when hot, gently fry the prawn pops, a few at a time, for a couple of minutes until the outside is a nice golden colour.

Chop the spring onion thinly and place in a small bowl. Heat 2 tbsp of annatto seed oil (or vegetable oil) and pour over the spring onion. Add the final teaspoon of fish sauce and a pinch of freshly ground black pepper. Arrange the prawn pops on a plate and drizzle this oil over them to serve.

Note: frozen, ready-cut sugar cane sticks are available in the large Vietnamese or Asian supermarkets. If you can't find them, use metal skewers or fresh lemongrass sticks.

Crab Cakes

This basic crab cake recipe makes for an easy and tasty snack. But we can't resist experimenting, so in the note below we've explained how you can add an authentic textured crust. The secret ingredient is *com*, a speciality found only in Hanoi, only in September, and from one single village alone! *Com* is sweet, young, green rice; harvested early, it is soft, bouncy and immensely fragrant. It is brought into the city by vagrant vendors carrying baskets across their shoulders or on their bicycles. If you want to try this version, you can find *com* in Asian supermarkets and online.

Serves 4 as a starter

300g minced pork
50g crabmeat
1 tbsp chopped shallots
2 tsp crushed garlic
2 tsp gia vi (or a mix of
   2 parts sugar, 1 part
   sea salt, 1 part ground
   black pepper, 1 part
   garlic powder)
1 tbsp fish sauce
1 tsp sugar
1 tsp freshly ground
   black pepper
2 tbsp water
2 tsp vegetable oil, plus
   more for frying
1 egg
125g com rice (optional)

In a bowl, mix the minced pork and crabmeat with the shallots, garlic, gia vi, fish sauce, sugar and pepper.

Add 2 tsp of oil to the paste and continue mixing.

Crack the egg and add to the bowl, mixing well.

Using your hands, form the mixture into roughly 10 little patties.

In a frying pan or wok, heat about 2cm of oil on a medium-high heat. When hot, gently fry the crab cakes in batches until golden.

Note: if you want to make this with the young green *com* rice, take 125g of *com* and soak in just enough hot water to cover it. After about 10 minutes the rice will be plump and should have soaked up most of the water. Drain the rice of any remaining water. Mix half of the rice into the meat mixture and spread the other half out on a flat surface to roll the patties in before frying them.

Chinese Leaf Pork Dumplings

Pork dumplings wrapped in cabbage leaf are one of my mother's oldest recipes. I ate this dish every winter as a child in Hanoi. Even when I moved abroad, my mother still made it every winter holiday when I flew home. Now when I miss my mother, I cook these dumplings.

In this recipe, we've used Chinese leaf for its sweetness and softness, but savoy cabbage works just as well.

Serves 4 as a starter

1 Chinese leaf
100g chestnut mushrooms
200g minced pork
1 tsp chopped garlic
1 tsp chopped shallot
*1 tsp freshly ground
  black pepper*
1 tbsp fish sauce
Chilli sauce, to serve

Peel the Chinese leaf, cut out the hard white stem and chop this finely.

In a steamer (or a metal colander or steamer basket set over a pan of simmering water), lightly steam the leaves so they are soft and foldable but not overcooked.

Chop the chestnut mushrooms finely, then mix with the chopped white stem of the Chinese leaf. Work the pork mince into the mix and season with the garlic, shallot, pepper and fish sauce.

On a chopping board or clean surface, lay out the steamed Chinese leaves, spoon a dessertspoonful of the pork and mushroom mix into a single leaf, then fold the leaf over.

Repeat until you have used all the mixture. It should make roughly 10 dumplings.

Steam the dumplings in a steamer (or a metal colander or steamer basket set over a pan of simmering water) for 5–8 minutes, until cooked.

Serve the dumplings warm or cold with some chilli sauce drizzled on top.

Pomegranate and Pear Sweet Pudding

Vietnamese food is almost always dairy free, as we use soy milk or coconut milk instead of cow's milk. So our desserts are quite different to Western ones. We have one typical pudding we call *che*, which is usually tapioca bubbles simmered for a long time with fruit. We have made our recipe quicker and fresher by using simple tapioca flour as well as fresh fruit that hasn't been stewed to death. You can use just about any fruit – apple, pear or mango – to achieve a mild, fragrant sweetness.

Serves 4

3 tbsp tapioca flour
500ml water
250ml coconut milk
115g sugar
1 pomegranate
1 pear
Ice cubes, to serve (optional)

In a saucepan, dissolve the tapioca flour in the water, add the coconut milk and bring to the boil. Reduce the heat to medium-low, and stir in the sugar.

Cut the pomegranate in half and remove the seeds. Peel and core the pear, then chop into tiny pieces of a similar size to the pomegranate seeds.

Stir the fruit pieces into the tapioca and coconut milk mixture.

Serve warm or leave to cool and serve cold over ice.

Clementine Jasmine Iced Tea

Kumquat iced tea is a stalwart on the menu at the Banhmi11 market café, No.101, in Shoreditch, which opened in 2012. The moment had arrived to spread our wings beyond solely doing street food. Kumquat is a rare fruit but, for the Vietnamese, this winter citrus is auspicious. The kumquat pot plant occupies an honourable place in Vietnamese homes, together with cherry blossom branches, to celebrate New Year. Here we've used clementine, the UK's winter-fruit equivalent.

Serves 2

200ml strong black tea
    or jasmine tea
2 clementines
4 tbsp sugar
Crushed ice, to serve

To garnish:
2 wedges clementine
2 mint leaves

Brew the tea, then strain through a tea strainer into a jug and leave to cool.

Take 2 tall glasses and squeeze the juice from a clementine into each glass. Add 2 tbsp of sugar to each glass and mix well until the sugar dissolves.

Add the cooled tea and some crushed ice. Garnish each glass with a wedge of clementine and a mint leaf.

Crème Caramel

Banhmily is what we call our staff at Banhmi11. We are a group of workaholics and dreamers, on a somewhat chaotic mission, but somehow we manage to hold everything together, bound by our shared love of food.

This crème caramel recipe came from a challenge we set when testing recipes for our dinner menu. Anh would test a different savoury recipe every day, while Tu Anh, her junior namesake, would test a dessert.

The condensed milk really brings out the sweetness in this dish, although you could equally well use fresh milk or cream.

Serves 6

1 x 397g can condensed milk
2 cans hot water (794g measured in above can)
4 egg yolks
3 tbsp sugar
¾ tsp vanilla extract
¼ tsp salt
150ml Caramel Water (see p.194)

Preheat the oven to 180°C/gas 4.

Empty the condensed milk into a bowl. Use the can to measure out double the amount of hot water, and add to the bowl. Stir so the condensed milk is mixed into the hot water.

Whisk together the egg yolks and sugar and pour into the milk. Mix well.

Add the vanilla and salt.

Strain the mixture through a coarse mesh strainer lined with cheesecloth to remove any lumps, so that the crème caramel has a smooth, silky texture.

Make the Caramel Water as per the instructions on p.194 and pour into the bottom of 6 ramekins. Gently pour the custard on top of the Caramel Water in each of the 6 ramekins.

Place the ramekins in a water bath (or in a roasting tin with enough water to come two thirds of the way up the tin). Bake in the oven for 25 minutes or until set.

Leave to cool, then put in the fridge for about 2 hours to set, before serving.

CHAPTER TWO

SOURNESS

AND

Change

The idea of a sour flavour might well bring to mind grimaces and sharp acidity. This is a misconception. It might not have the instant gratification of sweetness, but sourness is, in our opinion, the most nuanced flavour. There is the delightful light sourness of a Cox's apple, the fragrant freshness of lime, and the sharp acidity of vinegar, to name but a few. Sourness tempered with sweetness is widely used in Vietnamese cooking – from classic sweet and sour soup to zingy salads.

When Anh came to England to study aged 16, and when I moved to Sweden with my family aged 12, we experienced entirely new sour flavours: piquant Bramley apple crumbles; deceptively sour fragrant quinces; balsamic vinegar's sweet acidity; piercingly tart Swedish gherkin. All of these new taste sensations coincided with the upheaval of moving to a new school and a new country.

For us, sourness is the flavour of change. Change brings renewal, and when balanced with familiarity – like the marriage of sour with sweet – good things tend to happen. A midwinter red cabbage salad, sprinkled with hot mint defies winter's dullness with its colour and flavour (see p.86).

During our first year away from Vietnam, Anh and I endured terrible school meals and, for the first time, we realised the need to cook if we were to control our enjoyment of food. Nothing we saw, smelt or tasted at school really satisfied us, and this hunger made cooking an obsession for us. We took change into our own hands.

Everyday Cooking
(An Com)

When Banhmi11 stopped feeling like a hobby and began demanding our full-time attention, Anh quit her job. No fanfare, just a quiet acceptance that sometimes we choose our vocation and sometimes it chooses us. We recruited our first interns, who helped out with the admin, and a lot more besides – removing rubbish, testing menus, ferreting out ingredients, endlessly peeling garlic and squeezing lemon juice.

Crammed together in our kitchen-cum-office, we made lunch together. This was a daily exercise in improvisation. We stir-fried beef, instead of grilling it as on our market stall, and served it with vermicelli noodles. When we had ribs left over from pork belly, we made broth and threw in leftover pineapple and tomato for a sweet and sour soup.

Our kitchen had only the most rudimentary equipment, the centrepiece of which was a second-hand Blue Seal oven and six-burner hob we picked up from a Turkish catering shop. All six burners were occupied with cooking *pho* broth or making *banh mi* fillings, so we had to use the electric rice cooker in the corner of the office. This turned out to be a useful lesson in the value of simple, everyday cooking methods.

We didn't expect the interns to come every day, but they did. We didn't expect to eat together every day, but we did. Today, those first interns still work with us and are some of our most valued staff.

Rhubarb and Okra Sweet and Sour Soup

Rhubarb has always fascinated us. When we see its crimson stalks at the farmers' market, it's as if it's asking to be picked up. We love our rhubarb crumble and tarts, but recently we also found a way of making rhubarb into a sweet and sour soup. Anh was rummaging in the fridge for ingredients we could salvage, and she came across a few rhubarb stalks. On a whim we cut the stalks into chunks and tossed them into a soup. The results were so beautiful we cooked the same soup three days in a row.

Serves 4

3 rhubarb stalks
4 tomatoes
½ pineapple
50g okra
1 tbsp vegetable oil
1 tsp crushed garlic
1 tsp gia vi (or a mix of
    2 parts sugar; 1 part
    sea salt, 1 part ground
    black pepper, 1 part
    garlic powder)
1.5l water
2 tbsp fish sauce
1 tsp sugar
1 tbsp chopped spring
    onion
1 tbsp chopped fresh
    coriander

Wash the rhubarb and cut into 3cm chunks.

Slice the tomatoes in half and cut each half lengthways into 3 or 4 slices.

Cut the pineapple into 2cm chunks.

Cut the okra in half and remove the seeds, then cut into 1cm rounds.

In a heavy-bottomed pan, heat the oil and stir in the garlic until the oil is fragrant, taking care not to burn the garlic.

Stir in the tomatoes and season with ½ tsp of the gia vi. Pour in just enough water to cover the tomatoes, and bring to the boil.

When the tomatoes are soft, add the remaining water and bring back to the boil. Add the rhubarb and cook until very soft.

Stir in the fish sauce, sugar and the remaining gia via.

About 15 minutes before serving, add the okra and pineapple.

Sprinkle with the spring onion and coriander, and serve.

Sweet and Sour Ribs with Pineapple Sauce

Sweet and sour is a classic pairing in Vietnam and more widely in Asia. Use a good, heat-retaining pan so you can get your ribs succulent and sticky. The lemon and apple juice add a mild acidity, which helps the meat come off the bones.

Serves 4

1kg pork loin ribs
250ml water
1 tsp salt
20g piece fresh ginger, peeled and sliced
4 tbsp vegetable oil
2 tbsp finely chopped garlic
6 tomatoes
2 tsp chopped shallot
½ pineapple, sliced

Marinade:
1 tbsp gia vi (or a mix of 2 parts sugar, 1 part sea salt, 1 part ground black pepper, 1 part garlic powder)
2 tbsp fish sauce
½ tbsp fresh lemon juice
½ tbsp finely chopped garlic
1 tbsp chopped shallot
100ml fresh apple juice
½ tbsp freshly ground black pepper

To garnish:
2 tbsp chopped spring onions
2 tbsp chopped fresh coriander

To prepare the ribs, bring the water to boil in a large pan with the salt and sliced ginger, then add the ribs and boil vigorously for around 5 minutes. Lower the heat to medium and cook for another 10 minutes, then remove the ribs to a large dish.

Pat the ribs dry with a paper towel.

Mix the marinade ingredients, pour over the ribs, cover and leave for about 20 minutes.

Heat 3 tbsp of the oil in a frying pan, then add the finely chopped garlic and toss until the oil is golden and fragrant (about 5 minutes). Carefully strain the garlic oil through a fine mesh sieve so you have just the oil without any pieces of garlic.

Pour the strained oil back into the frying pan, add the ribs and fry until the ribs are golden, crispy and fragrant from the oil. Remove and set to one side.

Chop the tomatoes in half and then cut each half into thirds.

In a pan, add the remaining 1 tbsp oil and the chopped shallot, and toss until the oil is fragrant. Then add the chopped tomatoes and sauté for 5–10 minutes until the tomatoes have softened. Taste the seasoning and adjust the fish sauce or sugar if necessary.

Add the fried ribs, reduce the heat to low and cover. Cook for 30 minutes or longer if you prefer the ribs softer. Ten minutes before serving, add the pineapple slices.

Garnish with the chopped spring onion and coriander and serve with rice or noodles.

Note: if you have a pressure cooker, this is the quickest and easiest way to cook the ribs. Once you have made the sauce, put the ribs into the pressure cooker, cover with sauce and cook for 30 minutes.

Temple Tofu

A few years ago we visited Phu Quoc, an island off the coast of Vietnam, for the first time. As we explored it we came across a temple. There was a feeling of stillness which drew us in and, before we knew it, we'd walked right through to the back of the building where we found a kitchen. A young monk was making a fresh batch of tofu, churning the soy milk until it coagulated, like butter. A couple of nuns were cooking on wood-fired stoves, preparing a communal meal of curried tofu with coconut milk. The monk started chatting to us, and we didn't go anywhere else that day…or the next.

He showed us how to make soy milk, and explained how to make tofus of variable softness. With each meal, we discovered completely new ways of cooking vegan food: from tofu salads to fried tofu with lemongrass. The food was so light, it lifted our spirits and we felt completely energised by the time we finally left the temple.

Recipe continued overleaf

Serves 4

500ml hot water
1 tbsp salt
1 tbsp vinegar or lemon
  juice
500g fresh firm tofu
200ml vegetable oil, plus
  2 tbsp
6 tomatoes
1 tbsp crushed garlic
2 tbsp gia vi (or a mix of
  2 parts sugar, 1 part
  sea salt, 1 part ground
  black pepper, 1 part
  garlic powder)
1 tbsp sugar
750ml water
2 lemongrass sticks, finely
  chopped
4 tbsp soy sauce
2 tbsp chopped coriander

Temple Tofu continued:

Heat a large pan, add the hot water, salt and the vinegar or lemon juice, and bring to the boil.

Add the tofu and boil for 5–7 minutes, then drain the tofu, transfer to a chopping board and leave to cool.

When the tofu is cool, cut it into 2cm × 3cm chunks and use a paper towel to pat it dry. It's important that the tofu is dry so it will be nice and crispy later.

In a frying pan, heat the 200ml of oil over a medium heat. When the oil is hot, add the tofu pieces in batches so they are submerged in the oil. When you see the bottom of the tofu turning yellow and crispy, turn it over so it cooks evenly.

Rest the fried tofu on a plate lined with a paper towel to soak up the excess oil.

Meanwhile, chop the tomatoes into chunks (about 6–8 chunks per tomato).

In a heavy-bottomed pan, heat the remaining 2 tbsp of oil, then add the crushed garlic and toss for about 1 minute until fragrant. Add the chopped tomatoes and toss again for about 5 minutes.

Add the gia vi and the sugar and cook for another 5 minutes over a medium heat, until the tomatoes soften slightly.

Pour in the 750ml water, add the lemongrass and continue to cook for another 10 minutes.

Add the tofu to the pan, then stir in 2 tbsp of the soy sauce and cook for another 10 minutes. Now add the remaining soy sauce and turn the heat down to low. Continue to simmer the tofu for another 15 minutes.

Sprinkle with chopped coriander and serve with steaming hot rice or noodles.

Prawn Tamarind

This dish dates back to our first supper clubs. Once our stall was going strong on Broadway Market we began hosting pop-up supper clubs in local restaurants. These were great fun to cook for, as the guests would take pleasure in each dish as it appeared. This recipe shows how a good sauce can make a dish. With sauces, cooks can let their imagination run free and Anh is always coming up with new concoctions.

Serves 2

Tamarind sauce:
20g seedless tamarind pulp,
  cut from a slab (see p.201)
4 tbsp hot water
2 tbsp sugar
2 tbsp fish sauce
1 tsp finely chopped
  lemongrass

Prawns:
150g fresh prawns, peeled
1 tbsp vegetable oil
1 tbsp crushed garlic
1 tsp chopped shallot

To garnish:
2 spring onions, sliced
A few sprigs coriander

In a small bowl, soak the tamarind pulp in just enough hot water to cover it, for 10–20 minutes, until it becomes soft. Strain the juice into a mixing bowl. Stir in the sugar, fish sauce and lemongrass or if you want a slightly sourer or sweeter sauce, adjust the quantities according to taste.

To cook the prawns, heat the oil in a frying pan or wok and sauté the crushed garlic and chopped shallot. Stir in the prawns, turning them frequently. When they start to turn pink, add the tamarind sauce and simmer for a couple of minutes.

Garnish with slices of spring onion and sprigs of coriander.

Photo overleaf

Festive Cooking
(An Qua)

Vegetables are plentiful in Vietnamese cooking and fresh herbs accompany every dish. Nevertheless, strictly vegetarian dishes are hard to find. We might make a simple fried tofu but then pair it with a fish sauce dipping sauce. It's unthinkable to omit fish sauce in Vietnam – like trying to cook Italian without olive oil.

There is something frugal about purely vegetarian dishes. In Vietnam the only true vegetarians are the small Buddhist population. We've always found it amusing to see 'vegetarian' *pho* on menus in Vietnamese restaurants, when most of the time, chicken stock is probably cheekily used. So we set out to cook a really good vegetarian broth, without using esoteric ingredients like seaweed. Surprisingly, we didn't need to look far, as any British root vegetable – parsnip, celeriac, swede, carrots or turnip – makes for a really good stock (see p.193). Just add a couple of Vietnamese essentials: a contrast of flavours, some fresh herbs, a kick of chillies, and you have an ingenious vegetable soup.

Sweet and Sour Tofu Noodle Soup

Serves 2

*1l vegetable stock (or
home-made vegetable
broth, see p.193)
1 pack rice noodles
3 tomatoes
100g pineapple chunks
200g fresh firm tofu, diced
1 tbsp soy sauce
1 tbsp chopped spring
onions
1 tbsp chopped fresh
coriander*

Here the sweet and sour complement each other, adding
interest rather than taking anything away from the dish.

Heat 1 litre of vegetable stock in a large pan.

Cook the noodles according to the packet instructions.

Cut the tomatoes in half, then each half into thirds.

Bring the broth to the boil and add the tomatoes, pineapple and tofu
pieces. Season with 1 tbsp of soy sauce, or to taste.

Divide the noodles between 2 bowls, then pour the broth over them.
Sprinkle with the chopped spring onions and coriander, and serve.

Social Cooking
(An Choi)

A crisp, mild sourness, balanced out with sugar and spiced up with chillies, is a simple formula for fail-safe salad dressings. Salads are some of the most little known yet enjoyable Vietnamese dishes for Western tastes. We don't actually eat leaves raw – fresh herbs being an exception – so the vegetables are usually lightly pickled to infuse the flavours. Salads feature prominently on celebratory menus, and whether it's a New Year celebration or the christening of a child, their herb-filled lightness makes for a snacky respite in an otherwise heavy meal.

Papaya Salad with Crispy Anchovies

Anh's favourite streetside stall, next to a bustling market, served papaya salad. This salad usually comes with beef, prawns or even grilled quail. We tried several variations of our own before hitting on the idea of using deep-fried dried anchovies. The crisp texture of the anchovies contrasts beautifully with the papaya. This is delicious served with the Garlic, Lime and Chilli Dipping Sauce on p.198 tossed over it like a dressing. Top with a sprinkling of fresh herbs and ground peanuts.

Dried anchovies are available from most Asian supermarkets, and we use a quick frying technique to make them crispy again.

Serves 4

1 green papaya, about 300g
1 carrot
1 tsp salt, plus a pinch
Vegetable oil for deep-frying
30g dried anchovies
Pinch of sugar
1 tbsp chopped rau ram or coriander, plus extra sprigs for garnishing
1 tbsp chopped mint leaves, plus extra sprigs for garnishing
1 firm mango
100g peanuts, crushed

Dressing:
Garlic, Lime and Chilli Dipping Sauce (see p.198)

Wash and peel the papaya and carrot. Rinse the papaya in cold water to remove the resin from the green fruit, then cut the fruit in half and remove the seeds. Shred the papaya and carrot into long slithers using a grater or food processor.

Soak the shredded papaya and carrot in cold water with the 1 tsp of salt for 10 minutes. Drain and leave to dry.

Fill a small, heavy-bottomed pan with oil to 2cm deep and heat. To test if the oil is hot enough, drop in an anchovy, and if it sizzles, the oil is ready. Deep-fry the anchovies, a few at a time, until slightly brown, and carefully remove to a plate lined with a paper towel to drain.

Tip the anchovies into a bowl. Sprinkle a pinch of sugar and salt over them and shake well.

In a large bowl, mix the shredded papaya and carrot with the chopped herbs. Peel and shred the mango and add it in.

Dress the papaya with the Garlic, Lime and Chilli Dipping Sauce on p.198. Transfer to serving plates. Top with the anchovies and sprinkle the crushed peanuts over. Garnish with a few extra sprigs of herbs.

Note: green papaya is a special variety found in Asian supermarkets. You can substitute with kohlrabi or even green apples. But don't use yellow papaya as it will disintegrate.

Beef Carpaccio with Red Onion and Herb Salad

I didn't believe Anh when she first told me that we could 'cold cook' meat. The first time she prepared this dish I made her sear the beef again, almost turning it into a stir-fry. If you can slice the beef very thinly, it's best eaten raw — simply steeped in the lime and chillies. But if you prefer your meat more rustic and thick-cut, flash-fry it for a moment before dressing it.

Serves 4

300g sirloin steak
2–3 red onions
Juice of 3 limes
200g beansprouts
2 tbsp chopped coriander
5 tbsp Garlic, Lime and
   Chilli Dipping Sauce
   (see p.198)
1 tbsp crushed peanuts
2 red chillies, chopped

To garnish:
A few sprigs coriander
4 lime wedges

Cut the beef into very thin slices. This is easy to do if you part-freeze it first (see p.209).

Prepare the red onions, following the red onion pickle recipe on p.195, but soak the onions in the hot water for a shorter amount of time – a couple of minutes – before steeping in the pickle brine for a few minutes. They need to be crunchy here as we will be serving them right away as a salad rather than letting them pickle.

Squeeze the juice from the limes into a bowl.

Dip the thin slices of beef in the lime juice. This will 'cook' the beef. Even without heat, the beef should turn from the bright red colour of raw meat to the light brown colour of seared meat. Layer them over a large serving plate.

Take the red onion out of the pickle brine, and scatter over the plate of beef along with the beansprouts and chopped coriander.

Make up the Garlic, Lime and Chilli Dipping Sauce on p.198 and pour over the salad.

Sprinkle the peanuts and chilli over the salad. Garnish with sprigs of coriander and a wedge of lime on the side.

Shredded Chicken, Red Onion and Herb Salad

This shredded chicken salad is a taste of summer. The banana blossom is optional but it adds a wonderful earthy taste. The banana tree is widely used in Vietnamese cooking. It's an example of Vietnamese resourcefulness as the leaves are used to wrap around sticky rice or cover fish on the grill, while the blossom is made into a salad, and even the porous banana trunk is sliced thinly to serve with fresh herbs.

Serves 4

2 chicken thighs, boneless
Pinch of salt
50g fresh ginger, peeled
   and thinly sliced
2 red onions
5 tbsp Garlic, Lime and
   Chilli Dipping Sauce
   (see p.198)
2 tbsp chopped rau ram
   or coriander, plus a few
   sprigs for garnishing
1 tbsp crushed peanuts
100g shredded banana
   blossom (optional)

In a pan, add the chicken thighs, a pinch of salt and the slices of fresh ginger. Cover with water, bring to the boil and then simmer on a low heat for about 25 minutes, or until the chicken is cooked.

Remove the chicken thighs and soak briefly for a couple of minutes in a bowl of cold water, then drain and shred the chicken into thin strips.

Prepare the red onions, following the red onion pickle recipe on p.195, but soak the onions in the hot water for a shorter amount of time – a couple of minutes – before steeping in the pickle brine for a few minutes. They need to be crunchy here as we will be serving them right away as a salad rather than letting them pickle.

In a mixing bowl, mix together the red onions and chicken.

Make up the Garlic, Lime and Chilli Dipping Sauce on p.198 and pour over the onions and chicken.

Sprinkle the peanuts and chopped herbs over the salad, and garnish with a few extra sprigs.

Note: for a crunchy texture and earthy flavour add shredded banana blossom, which is available all year round in Asian supermarkets. You can also buy whole banana blossoms and serve individual portions in these beautiful big red petals to wow your guests.

Red Cabbage and Beansprout Salad with Herbs

This very simple winter salad makes a sumptuous companion to stews and braised dishes. The sweetness of the Caramelised Braised Pork Belly recipe on p.26 cries out for the contrasting acidity of this salad. It also works well as a crispy snack with rice crackers.

Rice vinegar and fruit vinegars such as cider vinegar are fine to use here, but avoid malt, wine and balsamic vinegar as they are too acidic.

Serves 4

½ red cabbage
2 tsp salt
1 tsp sugar
1 tbsp vinegar
100g beansprouts
1 bunch rau ram or mint,
    chopped

On a chopping board, hold the red cabbage firmly and use a sharp knife to grate off thin slivers.

In a bowl, soak the red cabbage slivers in hot water with 1 tsp of the salt for 5 minutes. Drain and leave to dry.

Place the red cabbage in a bowl and sprinkle with the remaining 1 tsp of salt and the sugar. Squeeze the cabbage with your hand so that the sugar and salt is absorbed into the cabbage.

Add the vinegar. Use your hand again to squeeze the cabbage so the flavours are absorbed fully.

Add the beansprouts and chopped rau ram or mint, and toss well before serving.

Scrambled Egg with Tomato and Spring Onion

This is our emergency recipe, for when the fridge is empty but we are hungry and need a meal in 10 minutes. We dash to the corner shop for a carton of eggs, a couple of tomatoes and a bunch of spring onions. This is simple to cook but delicious. It is also a great recipe for a weekend breakfast.

Serves 1

1 egg
½ tsp gia vi (or a mix of
    2 parts sugar, 1 part
    sea salt, 1 part ground
    black pepper, 1 part
    garlic powder)
½ tsp fish sauce
1 tomato
1 tbsp vegetable oil
1 tbsp chopped spring onion

In a bowl, whisk the egg and season with the gia vi and fish sauce.

Cut the tomato in half and then cut each half into thirds.

Heat the oil in a small, heavy-bottomed pan, then add the tomato and stir until soft.

Pour the egg mixture over the tomatoes, and cook on a medium-low heat, stirring frequently.

Remove from the heat while the egg is still moist and fluffy.

Sprinkle with chopped spring onion and serve with rice or bread.

CHAPTER THREE

SPICINESS

AND

Adventure

Many people assume that Vietnamese food is spicy, like Thai. But Vietnam is a long, thin country and its cooking varies hugely from one region to another. In the south and centre, chillies are used liberally, but in the north, where we come from, strong spices are used sparingly. We favour subtle sweetness, which is why we Hanoians do the best *pho*.

Chillies are the loudest spice; they're small but attention-seeking. However there are other spices which deserve more recognition than they get. Ginger brings a warm, fragrant spiciness to dishes; we often pair it with seafood because its elegant scent eliminates any fishy odour. Lemongrass, in marinades, stir-fries and noodle soups, adds a subtly spicy heat. Black pepper is the most versatile spice, packed with aroma that transforms a dish.

It wasn't until we moved to New York that we really got into spicy food. We were both in our twenties, in our first jobs and truly independent for the first time in our lives. We lived in a fifth-floor walk-up apartment in Long Island City with a view of the Manhattan skyline across the bridge. On summer nights, we would pull up the window and sit on the fire escape with our feet dangling, mesmerised by the lights of that iconic skyline.

We spent that whole year eating. We tried the midtown lunch scene's chi-chi sandwiches, ate roasted chestnuts after skating in Bryant Park, nibbled seafood pancakes in late-night Koreatown, had tea on the Bergdorf Goodman store rooftop looking out towards Central Park, spun cotton candy at St Mark's Place, and picked Sunday dim sum from the steaming trolleys in Flushing.

Most exciting of all were Saturdays: we'd ride the N train to Canal Street on a pilgrimage to the famous Paris Deli, renowned for its Vietnamese *banh mi*. We'd order the Number 1 Special, together with a bubble tea, and stock up with three or four baguettes for the rest of the weekend.

Paris Deli epitomised the New York attitude to food – it was less about taste and more about abundance. It was always open, always busy, and there were so many options to choose! The *banh mi* of our childhood in Vietnam had just a smear of pâté, a little butter, scraps of roast pork and some sprigs of coriander. Now Paris Deli showed us that *banh mi* should come in a dozen flavours, from turkey and cheese to sardine. It must also be very spicy and served with a generous dollop of the great Vietnamese-American success story, Sriracha sauce, with the rooster on its bottle. This loud food was a far cry from what we grew up with in the isolated Vietnam of the 1980s.

I am grateful to Paris Deli, because without its massive store in Chinatown, the idea of *banh mi* as an urban food would never have captured my imagination. And I'm grateful we came to London, because in New York we might never have seen the world in daylight and got off the merry-go-round of consumption, to start being creative.

Everyday Cooking
(An Com)

After our last year at Oxford University, Anh and I went on a road trip to Tibet. We wanted to learn how spices like ginger and chillies were used in different ways in everyday cooking across Asia. To reach the Tibetan capital, Lhasa, we crossed the Himalayan mountain range, which was more spectacular than I could have imagined. We spiralled through mountain passes in heavy snow, which opened out onto immense spaces. We saw herds of antelope, and yaks herded by nomadic shepherds whose temporary huts were covered with prayer flags, and we passed pilgrims on foot coated in dust.

One night we stayed in a Tibetan home. I can't remember what it looked like, except that the bed was a concrete platform with an oven underneath and colourful flowery blankets on top. But we both clearly remember our breakfast the next morning. We were fed a potato noodle soup with a steamy vegetable broth, served in cast-iron pots. I noticed the slices of ginger floating around in the massive soup bowl and it struck me that even though we'd never had potato noodle soup before, all our lives we had slurped great-tasting broth fragrant with ginger. Ginger is the ideal ingredient for simple, everyday cooking. Unlike other spices, its heat is not burning, but comfortingly warm and cleansing.

Watercress, Clam and Ginger Soup

Clams are possibly the easiest way to a great seafood stock. We use them to make stock for soups and hotpots. The warmth of ginger balances the seafood, which is considered a 'cold' food.

Serves 4

300g clams
1.2l water
Pinch of salt
50g piece fresh ginger,
    peeled and thinly sliced
2 tsp fish sauce
1 tsp gia vi (or a mix of
    2 parts sugar, 1 part
    sea salt, 1 part ground
    black pepper, 1 part
    garlic powder)
1 bunch watercress,
    trimmed and chopped

Rinse the clams to remove any grit.

In a large pan, boil the clams in the water with a pinch of salt. Add the sliced ginger and cook until the clams open, which means they are cooked.

Season with the fish sauce and gia vi and add the watercress a couple of minutes before serving. Discard any clams that don't open.

Spicy Root Vegetable Soup

Winter root vegetables often seem so impenetrable with their thick skin and weight that we're tempted to leave them in the vegetable rack. We favour delicate leafy vegetables that demand we do something with them while their goodness lasts. Yet root vegetables are packed with flavour, and where we once might have used a couple of prawns or a cup of chicken stock to cook leafy vegetables, now we often simply use the stock from celeriac and swede. They make the perfect vegetarian broth and here, where they offset the sweet tomato and the sour pineapple, they hit just the right note.

Serves 2

400g celeriac
300g swede
3–4 vine tomatoes
1 tsp gia vi (or a mix of
　2 parts sugar, 1 part
　sea salt, 1 part ground
　black pepper, 1 part
　garlic powder)
1 tsp chopped small red
　chillies
200g pineapple, cubed

Cut the celeriac and swede into cubes about 3cm thick.

Chop the tomatoes in half, and then cut each half into thirds.

Bring water to boil in a large pan, add the celeriac and swede and simmer on a medium heat for 20 minutes, until soft. If you have more time, you can leave it to cook for longer on a low heat.

Season with the gia vi and add the tomatoes and chilli.

Just before serving, add the pineapple cubes.

Tofu with Lemongrass and Chilli

At the island temple where we learned to cook Temple Tofu (see p.70) we learned more ways to cook tofu than we had ever thought possible. This recipe is for a traditional fried tofu, but we have breaded it with chopped lemongrass and and chilli to give it an extra dimension.

Serves 4

500ml hot water
1 tbsp salt
1 tbsp vinegar or lemon
    juice
500g fresh firm tofu
2 lemongrass sticks, finely
    chopped
200ml vegetable oil

Dipping sauce:
2 tsp soy sauce
½ tsp chopped fresh chillies,
    or to taste

Pour the hot water into a large pan, add the salt and vinegar or lemon juice, and bring to the boil.

Add the tofu and boil for 5–7 minutes, then drain the tofu, place on a plate and leave to cool. This will revive the tofu and clean it of any sourness.

When the tofu is cool, cut it into 2cm x 3cm chunks and use a paper towel to pat it dry. It's very important that the tofu is dry so it will be nice and crispy later.

Use a small sharp knife to make slits in the tofu about 5mm deep so the lemongrass will stick to it.

Spread the chopped lemongrass on a plate, then coat the tofu with it, using your hands to rub it in the 'channels' that you have created with the knife.

In a frying pan, heat the oil over a medium heat. When the oil is hot, add the tofu so it's submerged in the oil. When you see the bottom of the tofu turning yellow and crispy, turn it over so it cooks evenly.

Make the dipping sauce by pouring the soy sauce in a bowl and add as much chilli as you are comfortable with.

Serve with rice, noodles or over a mixed green salad.

Pan-Fried Pork Belly with Black Pepper and Spring Onion

Pork belly is one of the most versatile cuts of meat and can be cooked in a variety of ways – such as steamed and used as a filling for summer rolls, or braised and eaten with rice. While our Caramelised Braised Pork Belly recipe (see p.26) needs a slow simmer, this pan-fried pork belly recipe is quick and the meat comes out crispy and with honeyed edges.

Serves 2

200g lean pork belly
1 tbsp vegetable oil
1 bunch spring onions,
    chopped

Marinade:
1 tsp freshly ground black
    pepper
½ tsp gia vi (or a mix of
    2 parts sugar, 1 part
    sea salt, 1 part ground
    black pepper, 1 part
    garlic powder)
1 tbsp fish sauce
1 tsp sugar
1 tsp crushed garlic
1 tsp chopped shallot

Slice the pork belly thinly and place in a dish.

Combine the marinade ingredients and pour over the pork. Cover and leave in the fridge for 15–25 minutes.

Heat the oil in a frying pan over a medium-high heat. Stir in the pork belly and turn the heat down to medium-low. Cover with a lid and cook for about 7 minutes, until the meat is soft and moist.

Remove the lid and toss the pork around vigorously until it's golden and crispy.

Scatter the chopped spring onions over the pork and stir for another 2–3 minutes. Serve immediately.

Shaking Beef with Black Pepper

Cubed beef steak is a popular dish in Vietnam because it goes perfectly with a draught beer, which is why it often appears on the menu in Vietnam's many watering holes. Here is Banhmi11's twist on this recipe. We serve it with home-made chips and a watercress salad, and it has wowed many a dinner guest. It's extremely easy to cook but, as with all steaks, make sure you ask your butcher for a nice, tender cut.

Serves 4

500g sirloin steak
2 tbsp vegetable oil
1 tsp crushed garlic
Black pepper, to taste

Marinade:
1 tsp chopped garlic
½ tsp gia vi (or a mix of
  2 parts sugar, 1 part
  sea salt, 1 part ground
  black pepper, 1 part
  garlic powder)
2 tbsp soy sauce
2 tbsp oyster sauce
2 tbsp fresh pear juice
1 tbsp fresh pineapple juice
1 tbsp freshly ground black
  pepper
1 tbsp vegetable oil

To serve:
Lettuce or watercress
Slices of pineapple
Sliced cucumber

Cut the steak into 2–3cm cubes.

Combine the marinade ingredients in a large dish. Add the beef cubes, cover and leave to marinate for up to 1 hour.

Heat the oil in a large wok over a high heat. Add the crushed garlic and toss until the oil is fragrant.

Gradually add the marinated beef to the pan in small batches and toss for a couple of minutes, shaking the pan so the meat is evenly coated. Take care not to overcook it or it'll become very tough.

To serve, arrange the lettuce or watercress salad on serving plates with the pineapple slices and sliced cucumber. Top with the beef and sprinkle with black pepper.

Note: you can also thread the beef cubes onto skewers with sliced red or green peppers and then grill over charcoal for a tasty barbecue dish.

Wok-Fried Black Pepper Beef and Celery

In Vietnam we like the soft texture of celery leaves more than the crunchy stalks, which we rarely eat. But in this UK-friendly recipe you use the stalks. Using a wok means that the heat rises up the sides to maximise contact with the vegetables, plus the fragrance of caramelised garlic and onion is folded back into the food. If you don't have a wok, use a deep pan rather than a frying pan.

Serves 2

200g sirloin steak
100g celery
1 tbsp vegetable oil
½ tsp crushed garlic

Marinade:
1 tsp freshly ground black
   pepper
½ tsp gia vi (or a mix of
   2 parts sugar, 1 part
   sea salt, 1 part ground
   black pepper, 1 part
   garlic powder)
1 tsp sugar
1 tsp crushed garlic
1 tsp chopped shallot

Slice the beef as thinly as you can and place in a dish.

Chop the celery into 1cm slices.

In a bowl, combine the marinade ingredients and pour over the sliced beef. Cover and leave in the fridge for 15–25 minutes.

Heat the oil in a wok or deep-sided, heavy-bottomed pan. Add the garlic and stir vigorously until the oil is fragrant. Stir in the beef and flash-fry for 1–2 minutes. Add the chopped celery and continue to stir for a couple more minutes, depending on how you like your beef cooked. Serve immediately.

Beef Stewed with Ginger

This beef stew is a hand-me-down from Anh's mother. It is a speciality of her hometown in central Vietnam. This dish is as comforting to us as beef and Yorkshire pudding is to the British.

Serves 4

500g diced braising beef
1 tbsp vegetable oil
50g piece fresh ginger,
   peeled and sliced
200ml water

Marinade:
1 tbsp chopped garlic
½ tsp gia vi (or a mix of
   2 parts sugar, 1 part
   sea salt, 1 part ground
   black pepper, 1 part
   garlic powder)
2 tbsp soy sauce
2 tbsp oyster sauce
2 tbsp fresh pear juice
1 tbsp fresh pineapple juice
1 tbsp freshly ground black
   pepper
2 tbsp vegetable oil

In a large bowl, combine the marinade ingredients. Add the beef, then cover and leave in the fridge for 20 minutes.

Heat the oil in a flameproof casserole or large heavy-bottomed pan (one that has a lid), and add the beef and ginger. Stir quickly, then turn the heat down to low. Add 50ml of the water and cover. Simmer on a low heat. Check regularly and top up with 50ml of water each time the meat begins to look dry. Cook for about 30 minutes.

Serve with rice and greens.

French Beans with Garlic

Serves 2

200g French beans
1 tbsp vegetable oil
1 tsp crushed garlic
1 tsp fish sauce
1 tsp gia vi (or a mix of
  2 parts sugar, 1 part
  sea salt, 1 part ground
  black pepper, 1 part
  garlic powder)

This classic stir-fry with chopped garlic is for any meal and any time of the year.

Wash the French beans and break into pieces about 5cm long.

Heat the oil in a wok or frying pan. Stir in the garlic and French beans and cook for about 3 minutes, until the beans are cooked but still crunchy.

Season with the fish sauce and gia vi and serve immediately.

Roast Chicken with Honey, Black Pepper and Fish Sauce

Chicken holds a special place in Vietnamese food culture. It's often cooked on celebratory occasions. Before people sit down to eat, the chicken is offered to the spirits of the ancestors, and on New Year's Eve we eat chicken to give thanks for the past year.

This is our take on the Sunday roast. Here the chicken is basted in an intense peppery honey marinade which melds into the skin.

Serves 4

1 whole roasting chicken,
   about 1.5kg
250ml water

Marinade:
1 tsp crushed garlic
1 tbsp fresh lemon juice
1 tbsp fish sauce
1 tsp freshly ground black
   pepper
1 tbsp honey

Combine the marinade ingredients in a bowl.

Slit the skin of the chicken and rub in the marinade under the skin. Leave a small amount of marinade for basting the chicken later during cooking.

Wrap the chicken in clingfilm and leave in the fridge for about an hour.

Preheat the oven to 180°C/gas 4. When ready to cook, remove the chicken from its clingfilm. Pour the water into a baking tray, then place a roasting rack in the tray and sit the chicken on top. The water in the baking tray will produce steam to keep the chicken moist during cooking.

Roast the chicken in the oven for 1 hour 20 minutes, or until cooked. Every 15 minutes or so, brush the chicken with the remaining marinade to keep it moist. To check if the chicken is cooked, insert a sharp knife or metal skewer into the thickest part of one of the thighs, and if the juices run clear, the chicken is ready. If there are any pink juices, return the chicken to the oven for a further 10–15 minutes.

Serve with rice, a simple salad or, best of all, just like a traditional Sunday roast with all the trimmings.

Claypot Chicken with Ginger

There's a Vietnamese proverb that says chicken goes with kaffir lime leaves, and I'm not one to ignore age-old wisdom. Typically, this refers to a simple dish of steamed chicken that is neatly chopped and arranged on a plate with kaffir lime leaves spread on top. Here we've taken a classic braised dish – chicken with ginger – and adapted it by adding kaffir lime leaves. Our influence is the great many curries we've eaten since leaving Vietnam. The kaffir lime's coolness contrasts with the heat of the ginger, and lends a lush, tropical fragrance.

Serves 4

300g chicken thighs
  or drumsticks
1 tbsp vegetable oil
½ tbsp crushed garlic
50g piece fresh ginger,
  peeled and thinly sliced
4 tbsp water

Marinade:
1 tbsp crushed garlic
1 tbsp chopped shallot
1 tbsp vegetable oil
1 tbsp sugar
3 tbsp fish sauce
1 tsp gia vi (or a mix of
  2 parts sugar, 1 part
  sea salt, 1 part ground
  black pepper, 1 part
  garlic powder)
1 tbsp freshly ground
  black pepper
1 tbsp thinly sliced kaffir
  lime leaves, plus a couple
  for garnishing

In a large bowl, combine the marinade ingredients. Add the chicken, then cover and leave to marinate for up to 1 hour.

In a heavy-bottomed pan, heat the oil with the crushed garlic and the ginger and toss for 2–3 minutes until the oil is fragrant.

Add the chicken to the pan and toss for 2–3 minutes, then reduce the heat. Add the water and a little extra fish sauce if you need to, depending on your taste.

Simmer for around 45 minutes until the chicken is tender and the sauce has thickened. Make sure the chicken is thoroughly cooked before serving.

Transfer the chicken to serving plates and sprinkle with a few kaffir lime leaves.

Note: traditionally, this dish would be cooked in a clay pot rather than a pan, hence the name.

Salmon with Ginger Caramel

This has to be our favourite way of cooking salmon. Fish is a staple food in Vietnam, especially in the Mekong Delta, where it's eaten every day. In my second year at university, I worked in the countryside of the Delta as a volunteer for a few weeks. The fish there are firm, white and fatty, and they are simmered in caramel until tender and then spiced with chopped fresh chillies. Salmon is the ideal British equivalent: flavoursome and plump.

Serves 4

500g salmon fillets
50g thinly sliced fresh
   ginger
1 tbsp vegetable oil
200ml coconut milk
2 bird's-eye chillies, finely
   chopped

Marinade:
1 tbsp fresh lemon juice
1 tbsp gia vi (or a mix of
   2 parts sugar, 1 part
   sea salt, 1 part ground
   black pepper, 1 part
   garlic powder)
1 tbsp freshly ground
   black pepper
½ tbsp loose green tea
2 tbsp fish sauce
1 tbsp sugar
½ tbsp crushed garlic
2 tbsp chopped fresh ginger
1 tbsp chopped galangal
   (or 1 extra tbsp ginger)

Caramel sauce:
4 tbsp sugar
250ml water

Cut the salmon fillets into 4cm chunks. Combine the marinade ingredients in a bowl and rub into the salmon. Cover and leave in the fridge for about 20 minutes.

To make the caramel, place a heavy-bottomed pan over a medium heat, add the sugar and leave for 2–3 minutes without stirring. Turn the heat down to low and then stir constantly for about 2–3 minutes, until no grains of sugar are visible. The sugar will begin to melt and turn a brownish colour. Pay special attention to the colour of the caramel under the bubbles as it will darken very quickly. Just before it turns dark, add the water and cook until it boils. Don't worry if the sugar hardens upon contact with the water, as it will melt as it cooks, forming a caramel sauce.

Leave the caramel sauce to cool down for about 10 minutes, then stir in the sliced ginger.

Pour this sauce over the marinated salmon, then cover and leave in the fridge for another 20 minutes.

Now put a pan over a medium heat, add the vegetable oil and add the marinated salmon.

When the salmon starts to bubble, pour in the coconut milk and then taste the sauce again and add more fish sauce or sugar if necessary, before adding the chopped chillies.

Turn the heat down to low and leave the salmon to simmer for about 25 minutes, until the sauce has thickened and reduced by half.

Serve with rice and pickles.

Festive Cooking
(An Qua)

Nowhere in Vietnam is the tradition of festive cooking taken as seriously as in the old imperial city of Hue. Nestled in central Vietnam, Hue has its own very distinctive 'imperial' cuisine. Today, Hue has a feel of timeless tranquillity, and we have more of a sense of belonging there than in Hanoi where we grew up. Just before we opened our market café, No.101, in Shoreditch, we took a trip back to Hue.

Appropriately, we ate like kings on that trip. We sat in restaurants that looked as if they hadn't changed for 60 years. And we sat in coffee shops, the only girls in a roomful of men with their newspapers and cigarettes. Everything tasted delicious, insanely delicious.

There is one particular meal from that trip which is etched on my mind, Hue's best-known speciality: spicy beef noodle soup or *bun bo Hue*. Through coffee-shop chat, we heard the city's best spicy soup was made by an old lady on the patio of a nearby house. She'd been serving soup there since before 1975 – the feeling was her soup was 'true', unaffected by the vagaries of modern living. We were told we must go there at precisely 3pm.

We arrived at the patio at quarter to three. There was nobody around except an old man arranging chairs and we wondered if we'd come to the right place. We sat down at a small table. At a minute to three, three women ritualistically carried in two large stockpots of broth. One of the women, whom we guessed to be the maestro, took centre stage and sat down.

The old man took our orders and both Anh and I chose a bowl *day du*, or 'with everything', which usually means the most expensive dish on the non-written menu, with all the house specialities.

Our bowls arrived, full to the brim and steaming hot, fragrant with chilli and lemongrass, and layered with thin slivers of beef. It was one of the spiciest broths I've ever eaten, not because of the floating chilli oil so commonly used elsewhere, but because of the sparkling spiciness of slow-simmered lemongrass. We looked at each other and knew we were right to travel half the world to eat this soup. We finished our bowls and, even though we were full, ordered a third bowl to share. By the time we left the patio was packed with people, from families with young children to elderly people travelling from outside the city just for a bowl.

That little old lady was cooking something that appears on the menu of every Vietnamese restaurant in the world. She has been single-mindedly cooking the same dish for 40 years and she executed it with absolute flair. Back in London, the memory of that patio reassured me that something as makeshift as a market stall could be nurtured into an institution. If we, like the old lady, could cook simply and consistently, we might just be in with a chance.

Imperial Spicy Beef and Lemongrass Noodle Soup *(Bun Bo Hue)*

Serves 4

500g sirloin steak
2l beef stock (or home-
  made beef broth, see p.192)

Broth seasoning:
3 tbsp gia vi (or a mix of
  2 parts sugar, 1 part
  sea salt, 1 part ground
  black pepper, 1 part
  garlic powder)
5 tbsp fish sauce
1 bunch fresh lemongrass,
  crushed
1 large onion, chopped
2 tbsp diluted shrimp paste
  (see p.209)

Marinade:
1 tsp gia vi (or a mix of
  2 parts sugar, 1 part
  sea salt, 1 part ground
  black pepper, 1 part
  garlic powder)
2 tsp fish sauce
50g piece fresh ginger,
  peeled then grated or
  thinly sliced

If simple, clear *pho* is the signature food of the restrained north, then spicy *bun bo Hue* is the signature food of central Vietnam. The first time Anh and I ate it was when we lived in New York in our early twenties. Our northern palate wasn't accustomed to the spiciness and we struggled, with tears in our eyes, to finish our bowls. But we sought it out again time after time until we could make our own.

Slice the beef sirloin very thinly.

Bring the beef stock to the boil in a large pan or stockpot. Stir in the gia vi and fish sauce.

Add the lemongrass and the onion to the pan. Keep the broth topped up to the same level as when you started by adding a little hot water (do not add cold water as it will make the broth very cloudy).

Add the diluted shrimp paste to your broth a couple of teaspoons at a time over the next 20 minutes.

Combine the marinade ingredients in a bowl. Add the beef slices, then cover and leave in the fridge for about 20 minutes.

Prepare the chilli oil by heating the annatto seed or vegetable oil in a heavy-bottomed pan, then add the dried chilli flakes and chopped fresh chillies and toss for about 5 minutes so that the chilli completely dissolves in the oil.

Add a couple of tablespoons of this chilli oil to the broth, or to taste. You don't want the chilli oil to overpower the sweetness of the broth.

Taste the broth and adjust the seasoning if necessary.

Chilli oil:
50ml annatto seed oil (see
  p.191) or vegetable oil
2 tbsp dried chilli flakes
5 fresh bird's-eye chillies,
  chopped

To serve:
2 packs rice vermicelli
  noodles

To garnish:
Beansprouts, basil, round
  lettuce, lemon wedges and
  fresh chilli
Shredded morning glory
  and banana blossom
  (optional)

To assemble the bun bo Hue bowls:
Cook the noodles according to the packet instructions and divide between your bowls.

Arrange the rare beef on the noodles.

Bring the broth to a bubbling boil and ladle it into each bowl, distributing it evenly.

Arrange the garnishes on separate plates and serve alongside the *bun bo Hue* bowls.

Note: when you add the fish sauce and the diluted shrimp paste to the broth, pour a small quantity into a ladle and slowly dip the ladle in the broth in a circular motion until the ladle is fully submerged. This ensures that the pungent smell disperses and doesn't overwhelm the dish.

The original *bun bo Hue* recipe uses a stock from beef bones as well as pig's trotter and pork hock. This makes the broth very rich, like Japanese ramen broth.

Bun Bo Hue

Spicy Noodle Soup with Crabmeat and Prawn *(Banh Canh Cua)*

Of all the spicy food we ate in New York, our favourite was from a hole-in-the-wall restaurant we stumbled upon. We were driving through outer Queens, lost and hungry, when we spotted a small neon sign that read 'Little Saigon'.

We had no expectations. There was an old lady watching TV and a poster signed by the cast of *Cats* on the wall. We ordered the *banh canh cua*, a noodle soup with a red bisque-like broth made with chopped prawn and crabmeat. When it arrived, we gasped at the attention to detail. It tasted spicy but so sweet, like summer heat offset by monsoon rain.

We ate at Little Saigon every Sunday for the rest of that year. After a while the old lady began sharing her recipes for home-made yoghurt and mayonnaise for *banh mi*. She'd left Vietnam on a boat for Hong Kong and lived in a camp with three of her ten children for a few years. There she made yoghurt and traded it for other food. It transpired that when she came to New York she'd helped set up Paris Deli and had written their original *banh mi* recipes. We were struck with awe.

After we left New York, we visited Little Saigon whenever we returned on business. On our last visit she told us she was moving back to Saigon to live with her children. We've never ordered *banh canh cua* at a restaurant since. Instead we decided to make it ourselves as a tribute to Little Saigon.

Serves 4

500g fresh prawns,
    unpeeled
2l vegetable stock
    (or home-made vegetable
    broth, see p.193)
1 tbsp vegetable oil
1 shallot, finely chopped
300g white crabmeat

Chilli saté:
3 fresh bird's-eye chillies
½ tbsp salt
1 tbsp fresh lemon juice
½ tbsp thick (undiluted)
    shrimp paste

Broth seasoning:
2 tbsp diluted shrimp paste
  (see p.209)
2 tbsp gia vi (or a mix of
  2 parts sugar, 1 part
  sea salt, 1 part ground
  black pepper, 1 part
  garlic powder)
2 tbsp fish sauce
½ tbsp sugar
2 tbsp annatto seed oil
  (see p.191) (optional)
1 tbsp cornflour
4 tbsp water

To assemble ban canh cua
  bowls:
250g udon noodles
1 bunch spring onions,
  chopped
1 bunch coriander, chopped
1 small bunch rau ram or
  mint, chopped

Peel the prawns and keep the shells for the broth. Chop the prawns into small pieces.

Bring the vegetable stock to the boil in a large pan or stockpot. Add the prawn shells and leave to simmer, skimming off any bubbles that appear.

Heat the vegetable oil in a small frying pan and add the chopped shallot. Sauté for a minute so the oil is fragrant. Stir in the chopped prawns and the crabmeat and fry quickly. Remove to a plate and set aside.

Make the chilli saté by steaming the chillies. When the chillies are soft, finely chop them. Add the salt, lemon juice and thick shrimp paste.

Add the diluted shrimp paste to the broth. Stir in the gia vi, fish sauce and sugar. Then add the annatto seed oil (if using), followed by the chilli saté.

In a bowl, dissolve the cornflour in the water and stir into the broth, to thicken it. The broth should be quite thick, like a soup, but not as thick as a sauce.

To assemble the banh canh cua bowls:
Cook the noodles according to the packet instructions and divide between your bowls.

Arrange the prawns and crabmeat on the noodles.

Sprinkle the spring onions, coriander and rau ram or mint over the seafood.

Strain the broth then bring it to a bubbling boil and ladle it into each bowl, distributing it evenly.

Note: the traditional recipe from Hue uses pork bones for the broth, but for our vegetable-based alternative you can use almost any root vegetable.

Social Cooking
(An Choi)

If pubs are the heart of British social life, then in Vietnam the bars selling fresh draught beer, *bia hoi*, are where friendships are made, deals struck and secrets shared. The accompanying bar snacks, known as *nhau*, are the perfect pep-up on a long evening's drinking. Unusually for a girl, Anh grew up knowing this food from an early age.

Anh is the fourth daughter in a family of girls. After giving birth to three daughters in succession, when Anh's mother fell pregnant again she was convinced she was going to have a boy. She told her husband, who was stationed in Laos with the Army, to come home for the birth of his first son. When another girl was born, he just packed his bags and returned to duty, refusing to see her or give her a name. Anh's name, literally meaning 'big brother', was given to her by a family friend.

But like most fathers, Anh's had his own way of doting on her – his was to train her in sports. Every week he would take her to the Army Club's swimming pool. While she did laps, he would wait patiently for her at the *bia hoi* across the road where, with a cold beer in hand, he would munch on roasted peanuts and a bowl of fresh chillies.

Back then, *nhau* bar snacks were very simple. In modern Vietnam, they now come in every conceivable form, from lobster to hog roast.

Clams with Fresh Chilli and Lemongrass

Moules marinières, Vietnamese-style. These are perfect with crispy, thin-cut French fries.

Serves 4

1kg clams
250ml white wine
2 lemongrass sticks,
    chopped
2 fresh chillies, chopped

To garnish:
4–6 sprigs coriander
2–3 sprigs rau ram or mint

Soak the clams in a large bowl of cold water about 15 minutes before you want to cook them, to remove any sand or grit. Rinse well under cold running water.

Put the clams in a heatproof dish that will fit inside your wok or cooking pot. Pour the wine over them, and add the lemongrass and chilli.

Place the dish in the wok or cooking pot and pour in enough water to come halfway up the sides of the dish.

Place the wok or pot over a medium heat, cover and cook the clams for about 15 minutes.

Carefully remove the dish from the pot. Spoon into a serving dish, discarding any clams that don't open. Garnish with sprigs of coriander and rau ram.

Note: you can use pretty much any type of clams or mussels with this recipe.

Chargrilled Rice Paper with Quail Egg, Spring Onion and Chilli Flakes

In Vietnam the street-food stalls are huddled together. A drinks stall will set up next to a snacks stall, so customers can patronise both. Opposite the cathedral in Saigon, there's a small coffee place we love. One day we saw this curious dish being made at a makeshift stall nearby. That stall had the smallest footprint I had ever seen: the wife cooked from a small basket while the husband took the orders and the payment.

This is a quick and easy way to transform the rice paper commonly used for spring and summer rolls. Street-food ingenuity at its best!

Makes 4

4 sheets rice paper
4 quail eggs
1 bunch spring onions, chopped
Dried chilli flakes, to taste

If you are outdoors, use a charcoal grill or gas barbecue on a low flame. You can also cook this on a gas hob, using tongs to hold the rice paper about 15cm above the flame.

Using one sheet of rice paper at a time, roast it over a low flame for a couple of minutes, flipping it over frequently so the heat is evenly distributed.

Crack a quail egg on top and use a pastry brush in a circular motion to disperse the egg into a thin layer of omelette.

Sprinkle with some chopped spring onion and chilli flakes.

Take off the grill when the rice paper is crispy and golden brown.

Repeat with the remaining sheets and eggs.

Hot Ginger Tea

This is a favourite on our winter drinks menu. The comforting heat from this ginger tea has cured many colds and coughs, while the syrup's sweetness is just what we crave as we await the arrival of spring.

Makes 1 jar of ginger
   syrup

100g sugar
200ml hot water
200g fresh ginger, peeled
   and finely chopped

In a heavy-bottomed pan, melt the sugar on a medium-high heat. Stir with a wooden spoon so the sugar doesn't burn.

Once the sugar is brown and caramelised, pour in the hot water and cook for another 5 minutes, being sure to re-melt any sugar that hardens.

In a separate frying pan, sauté the ginger on a medium-low heat for 5 minutes until fragrant. Use a wooden spoon or chopsticks to toss the ginger so it doesn't burn.

Then pour the sautéed ginger into the caramel water and simmer on a low heat for 15 minutes.

Leave to cool, then pour the ginger syrup into a sterilised jar and it will keep refrigerated for 2 weeks.

To make hot ginger tea:
Brew a pot of strong black tea or roasted green tea.

In each cup, add 2 tbsp of ginger syrup, then pour the hot tea over the syrup.

Stir well and serve.

Note: to sterilise jars, wash them thoroughly in warm soapy water, then rinse in clean warm water. Allow them to drip-dry, upside down, on a rack in a medium oven for 5 minutes.

CHAPTER FOUR

BITTERNESS

AND

Perspective

Bitterness is a flavour of perspective. It's subjective, in that a strong espresso may be unbearably bitter for one person but full of depth for another. Likewise, celery and leek have bitter notes for the Vietnamese palate, whereas in Europe they provide the sweet base for a ragù or vegetable soup.

Our perspective changes as we grow up and develop more esoteric tastes. Coffee, dark chocolate and draught beer have incredible flavours, but they suit more mature taste buds than the sweet treats of childhood.

In our everyday lives too, bitterness has its downsides and its rewards. Growing a small business is a nerve-wracking experience – when the food gets burnt, or staff leave, equipment fails, or bills stack up. Or when all these disasters come at once, like that first winter after we'd just opened our market café at 101 Great Eastern Street, and I wondered if I'd been right to talk Anh out of her secure city job to follow this dream.

To get this bitterness into perspective, I thought about the first time I learned to cope with bitter loss. It was when I returned to Vietnam for my mother's funeral, less than six months after the phone call to say she had been diagnosed with cancer. After completing the funeral rituals, my sister, my father and I went on our first family holiday in 10 years to a small coastal town in Central Vietnam. For our first meal, I took them to a fantastic restaurant I'd discovered on an earlier holiday. I'd always imagined taking my mother, after she'd recovered, to eat in this place. It seemed impossible that it was just the three of us sitting there eating the house noodle soup. As I sipped the thick broth I let the flavours absorb me and my mind quieten. A love of food had been my mother's gift to me.

Back in London, I decided to quit my job and work at Banhmi11 full-time. I knew it would take time to grow the business, but I felt good would come of it. Day-to-day worries would always crop up but they would pass too. As Anh and I said to each other, we just have to cook one dish right, make one person happy, and it all starts to make sense.

Everyday Cooking
(An Com)

Cooking would be so easy if it was soothing all the time. But the truth is, cooking is tiring. It requires strong hands and stamina. Failures are exasperating, like the week we went through 23 permutations of home-made pâté before we nailed the perfect texture. And sometimes they are terrifying, like when we turned off the wrong stove and burned the chicken the night before market day. It's difficult to cook a good meal when you are tired, fed up or bored and yet the same meal seems simple when you are untroubled.

So the reason we cook, apart from providing fuel for our bodies, is because we care. Our mothers sometimes complained, yet every day they cooked a new meal as elaborate as the last, in solitary silence under a spinning fan. It's not just about enjoyment in the kitchen, it's what happens when we sit down together and share a meal. And this is never truer than when it comes to everyday cooking.

Spinach and White Crabmeat Soup

The mild bitterness of spinach combines with the sweetness of white crabmeat in this simple soup, which cooks in minutes and tastes scrumptious.

Serves 2

400ml water
100g white crabmeat
250g spinach
1 tsp fish sauce
1 tsp gia vi (or a mix of
  2 parts sugar, 1 part
  sea salt, 1 part ground
  black pepper, 1 part
  garlic powder)

Bring the water to the boil in a pan, add the crabmeat and boil for 10 minutes, until the broth is sweet.

Add the spinach and bring to the boil again.

Season with the fish sauce and gia vi, and serve.

Eggs with Chives

This recipe is for those days when you have to cook, but don't want to make an effort. It's super-quick to prepare. The egg's sweetness balances the bitterness of the chives which, according to Chinese medicine, has a cooling effect on the body and fights fatigue.

Serves 1

1 egg
½ tsp gia vi (or a mix of
  2 parts sugar, 1 part
  sea salt, 1 part ground
  black pepper, 1 part
  garlic powder)
½ tsp fish sauce
1 tbsp chopped chives
1 tbsp vegetable oil

In a bowl, whisk the egg and season with the gia vi and fish sauce. Stir in the chopped chives.

Heat the oil in a small frying pan. Pour the egg mixture into the pan and cook on a medium-low heat, stirring frequently.

Remove from the heat while the egg is still moist and fluffy.

Serve with rice or bread.

Prawn and Pork with Bitter Melon

The Vietnamese name for bitter melon, *kho qua*, translates as 'suffering has passed'. In Vietnam it is served as a reminder of tough times, and an encouragement that they, too, will pass.

Serves 4

3–4 wood ear mushrooms
4–6 dried shiitake
　mushrooms
50g fresh prawns, peeled
100g minced pork
1 tbsp fish sauce
½ tbsp gia vi (or a mix of
　2 parts sugar, 1 part
　sea salt, 1 part ground
　black pepper, 1 part
　garlic powder)
½ tbsp sugar
2 tbsp chopped spring onion
1 shallot, chopped
2 bitter melons

Soak the wood ear and shiitake mushrooms in hot water. After about 15 minutes, when the mushrooms have expanded, drain and rinse under cold water, then pat dry with a paper towel. Chop the mushrooms coarsely.

Chop the prawns coarsely.

In a mixing bowl, mix together the prawns, minced pork, mushrooms, fish sauce, gia vi, sugar, spring onion and shallot.

Pour hot water in a bowl and soak the bitter melons for 1 minute. This will make them slightly less bitter and they will turn a deep green colour.

Cut the melons into round chunks about 3cm thick. Use a spoon or small knife to scoop out the seeds. Now fill the melon rounds with the pork and prawn mixture.

Place the filled melon rounds in a heatproof dish that will fit inside your wok or cooking pot. Place the dish in the pot and pour in enough water to come halfway up the sides of the dish. Cover, and cook the melons for 20 minutes over a medium heat.

Serve with rice and/or vegetables or salad.

Note: bitter melon, or bitter gourd, is like a squash but with a distinctive flavour. You can buy it in Asian or Caribbean supermarkets.

Courgettes and Seared Sirloin

The courgette's edge of bitterness is preserved in this recipe by keeping it raw and real.

Serves 2

2 courgettes
250g sirloin steak

Dressing:
2 tbsp sugar
4 tbsp water
4 tbsp soy sauce
1 tsp grated fresh ginger
1 tbsp sesame oil
Juice of 1 clementine

To garnish:
1 tbsp chopped fresh
    coriander
1 tsp white sesame seeds
1 tbsp dried shallot
    (or toasted dried onion)

Cut the courgettes in half lengthways and use a vegetable peeler to shave off thin slices.

To make the dressing, put the sugar and water in a pan over a medium heat. When the sugar has completely dissolved, add the soy sauce, followed by the grated ginger and the sesame oil. Cut the clementine in half and squeeze the juice into the pan.

Soak the courgette slices in the dressing for 3–5 minutes then set to one side.

Cut the sirloin steak into thin slices and marinate in the dressing for 15 minutes, then lightly sear the sirloin in a frying pan or on a griddle.

Divide the sirloin slices between 2 serving plates.

Roll up the courgette slices and arrange alongside the seared sirloin.

Sprinkle the chopped coriander, white sesame seeds and shallot over the beef.

Squid, Leek and Pineapple Stir-Fry

This is perhaps one of the more unusual combinations for the Western palate. But it works beautifully. The sweetness of the pineapple, the bitterness of the leek, and the crunchy elasticity of the squid are delicious together.

Serves 2

1 leek
½ pineapple
1 tbsp vegetable oil
1 tsp chopped garlic
200g cleaned squid, cut into
  rings
1 tbsp fish sauce

Cut the leek in half lengthways and then chop into 3–5cm chunks.

Cut the pineapple into slices about 2cm thick.

Heat the oil in a wok or frying pan. Add the garlic and stir until the oil is fragrant and the garlic is lightly browned.

Stir in the chunks of leek and cook until almost done.

Stir in the squid and season with the fish sauce. Cook for 2–3 minutes until almost done. Finally, stir in the pineapple slices and cook for a couple of minutes on a high heat.

Remove from the heat and serve immediately.

Note: take care not to overcook the squid or it will become tough and rubbery.

Stewed Chicken with Dates and Goji Berry

When my mother was in hospital, we used to make her stew with goji berries. Goji berries, which are used in traditional Chinese medicine, can be found in health-food shops. In this recipe, the sweetness of the broth masks the bitterness of the herbs.

At one of our favourite street-food stalls in Hanoi, a woman stews chicken in cut-up soft drink cans. I find it amusing that such an important and ceremonial dish, one considered so curative, can be prepared in recycled soft drink cans. Another example of Vietnamese resourcefulness.

Serves 4

1 chicken, about 1.5kg
1 tbsp chopped fresh ginger
2 tbsp vodka
1 tbsp salt

Stuffing:
5–7 dates
1 tsp goji berries
10–15 lotus seeds (optional)
10–15 dry longan (optional)

Marinade:
3 tbsp fish sauce
½ tbsp sugar
1 tbsp gia vi (or a mix of
    2 parts sugar, 1 part
    sea salt, 1 part ground
    black pepper, 1 part
    garlic powder)
½ tbsp lemon juice

Preheat the oven to 180°C/gas 4. Wash the chicken under cold running water. Mix together the chopped ginger, vodka and salt and rub into the chicken. Rinse carefully.

Roast the chicken in the oven for 5–10 minutes to dry the skin.

Stuff the chicken's cavity with the dates, goji berries, and the lotus seeds and longan if you can find them.

Put the chicken in a large, heavy-bottomed pan. If you don't have a big enough pan, you can chop the chicken in half and put the stuffing on top.

Combine the marinade ingredients and pour over the chicken. Cook, covered, on a low heat for 1 hour 15 minutes.

Make sure the chicken is thoroughly cooked before serving. Test by inserting a metal skewer or sharp knife into the thigh joint, and if the juices run clear, the chicken is ready. If there are any pink juices, cook the chicken for a further 10–15 minutes.

This recipe is perfect served with rice for a restorative dinner whenever you feel run down.

Sea Bass Steamed with Beer

The Vietnamese have a special way of steaming fish so that it's packed with flavour. This is achieved primarily through the marinade, but also by replacing water with beer, so the fish benefits from the fermented flavour.

Serves 4

1 sea bass fillet, about 1kg
1 bunch dill
2 lemongrass sticks
100ml beer

Marinade:
1 tbsp chopped fresh ginger
½ tbsp crushed garlic
½ tbsp freshly ground
  black pepper
½ tbsp finely chopped
  lemongrass sticks
1 tsp sugar
2 tbsp fish sauce

Scale the fish and either cut into chunks or leave whole but slit the skin in 3 or 4 places.

In a bowl, mix together the marinade ingredients, rub into the fish and leave for 15–25 minutes.

Wash the dill and crush the lemongrass sticks with a rolling pin or the broad side of a knife.

Stuff the fish with the dill (save a couple of sprigs for the garnish) and lemongrass.

Put the beer in the bottom of a steamer and place the fish in a heatproof bowl above the beer. Steam the fish for about 10–15 minutes. (If you don't have a steamer, put the beer in a pan and the fish in a heatproof bowl, then place the bowl in a steamer basket or metal colander set above the pan.) About 5 minutes before the fish is ready (when it turns white), sprinkle a pinch of chopped dill on top.

This fish is great served with a summer salad.

Braised Aubergine

I can never resist plush, purple aubergines and always pick up a couple when I see them. I prefer smaller aubergines to the large, spongy types. Our mothers cooked aubergines with tofu, green plantains and shiso. This is Anh's take on the traditional recipe, so beloved in the repertoire of everyday Vietnamese cooking.

Serves 2

1 aubergine
3 tomatoes
1 tbsp vegetable oil
1 tsp chopped shallot
2 tbsp soy sauce
1 tbsp gia vi (or a mix of
    2 parts sugar, 1 part
    sea salt, 1 part ground
    black pepper, 1 part
    garlic powder)
150ml hot water
200g tofu
1 tbsp chopped fresh
    coriander
Shiso leaves (optional)

Cut the aubergine in half lengthways and then cut into slices about 2cm thick.

Cut the tomatoes in half and slice each half into 3 pieces.

In a heavy-bottomed braising pan, heat the oil and cook the shallot on a medium heat until the oil is fragrant. Add the tomatoes and stir frequently so they don't stick to the bottom of the pan. Season with the soy sauce and gia vi.

Add the aubergine, followed by the hot water, then turn the heat down and simmer for 20–30 minutes until the aubergine is soft.

Cut the tofu into 3cm cubes and add to the pan about 10 minutes before serving.

Sprinkle with the chopped coriander and shiso if you have some.

Note: firm tofu is easier to handle, though soft tofu will work fine in this recipe.

Festive Cooking (An Qua)

Duck Noodle Soup with Bamboo

Anh's mother is a real street-food veteran and this recipe takes inspiration from a dish she used to make at her *bun cha* stall. The sweetness from the duck soaks into the bitterness of the bamboo shoots, but when you tuck into the noodle soup, everything is enveloped in a wholly different, very earthy flavour.

Serves 6

1 duck
Salt for rubbing into duck
2l hot water
1 x 220g can bamboo
 shoots, drained

Marinade:
1 tbsp gia vi (or a mix of
 2 parts sugar, 1 part
 sea salt, 1 part ground
 black pepper, 1 part
 garlic powder)
½ tbsp freshly ground
 pepper
½ tbsp finely chopped fresh
 ginger
½ tbsp crushed garlic

Rinse the duck under cold water. Rub with salt and leave for 10 minutes. Then rinse again.

You can cook the duck whole or chop into quarters. Combine the marinade ingredients and rub into the duck's skin.

In a large pan or stockpot with a lid, bring the hot water to the boil. Gently add the duck and bring the water back to the boil to help the meat to cook evenly.

Put the lid on loosely, without covering the pan completely, so there is enough steam for the duck to cook and enough air to result in a clear broth.

Cook for 45–60 minutes, until the meat is tender but not too soft. Scoop out any scum or bubbles that appear on the surface.

Remove the meat and soak in a bowl of cold water for 5 minutes, then pat dry with a paper towel.

Strain the duck broth into a pan.

Broth seasoning:
1 large onion, unpeeled
300g piece fresh ginger,
   unpeeled
1 tbsp gia vi (or a mix of
   2 parts sugar, 1 part
   sea salt, 1 part ground
   black pepper, 1 part
   garlic powder)
1 tbsp fish sauce
1 tsp sugar

To assemble the bowls:
1–2 packs rice vermicelli
   noodles
8 spring onions, chopped
1 onion, sliced
1 bunch rau ram or mint,
   chopped

To serve:
1 bunch coriander, chopped
3 tbsp Ginger and Dill
   Dipping Sauce (see p.200)

For the broth seasoning, char the onion and ginger over an open flame on the hob, letting the skin burn for about 5 minutes, using tongs to rotate them occasionally, until they become softer and fragrant. Or grill them for 5 minutes, turning them over halfway. Then remove the charred skin, wash the onion and ginger and add whole to the broth.

Simmer the broth for 15 minutes then discard the onion and ginger. Season with the gia vi, fish sauce and sugar.

Add the bamboo shoots to the broth and bring it to the boil again.

To assemble the bowls:
Cook the noodles according to the packet instructions, then divide evenly between your bowls.

Add a layer of duck to each bowl – you can shred the meat or just chop and eat with the bone in.

Add a layer of spring onion, sliced onion and herbs.

Ladle the bubbling broth into each bowl.

Serve with the Ginger and Dill Dipping Sauce (see p.200).

Note: you can also use chicken for this recipe.

Social Cooking
(An Choi)

We grew up in Vietnam in the eighties, when doors were never closed and we were as close to our neighbours as our own relatives. The most joyous demonstration of this social living was the Lunar New Year of Tet, when the whole block would get together to cook an enormous Tet speciality cake on New Year's Eve. Over the three days of celebration, we would go from house to house, and each house would share a special dish they had cooked – things like sunflower seeds or candied winter melon, which were luxuries in those days. To many, the eighties might have seemed a bitter period for Vietnam. But for us two, it was the sweetest era, full of warmth and simplicity. Some might call us old romantics, to which I'd reply: it's a matter of perspective.

Grapefruit and Prawn Salad

This is a twist on a traditional Vietnamese recipe, which uses pomelo. Anh's mother would buy a farmer's basket full of pomelo at their ripest and store them in a nice cool place – under her bed to be precise – where they'd last through the winter. Pomelo has a gentler bitterness than grapefruit but the latter's juiciness makes for a great local substitute. Or you might want to try this with a pomelo from a Turkish, Polish or Asian grocer.

Serves 2

1 grapefruit
6 large prawns, peeled
    and cooked
4 tbsp Garlic, Lime and
Chilli Dipping Sauce
    (see p.198)
1 tbsp chopped rau ram
    or coriander

To garnish:
1 tbsp peanuts, crushed
1 tbsp dried shallot
    (or toasted dried onion)

Peel the grapefruit and be careful to remove all the white pith. Then separate the segments and take each segment out of its membrane. Try to preserve them in chunks if you can.

Mix together the Garlic, Lime and Chilli Dipping Sauce on p.198.

Put the grapefruit and prawns into a mixing bowl and stir in the dipping sauce.

Stir in the chopped rau ram or coriander.

Spoon onto a plate and sprinkle peanuts and dried shallot over the top.

Serve on its own or with rice crackers.

Note: this recipe lends itself to adaptation. You can use other seafood, such as scallops or squid, and different fresh herbs, such as mint.

Deep-Fried Calamari with Ale

When we go through a particularly unlucky spell – like the month when our delivery scooter got stolen in Brick Lane … and one of the kitchen staff badly cut his finger … and the stall's canopy at Berwick Street Market flew off and hit the environmental health officer – we Vietnamese eat a meal to erase the 'bad luck'. This meal typically involves squid, and here the mild bitterness of beer also helps drown our sorrows.

Serves 4

Batter:
250g tempura powder
  (or plain flour)
1 egg yolk
50ml beer
3 tbsp chopped fresh dill
2 tbsp chopped fresh ginger

Calamari:
400g frozen squid rings,
  defrosted
½ tbsp sugar
½ tsp freshly ground
  black pepper
¼ tbsp salt
Vegetable oil for frying

To serve:
Garlic, Lime and Chilli
  Dipping Sauce (see p.198)
2 lemons, cut into wedges

To make the batter, put the tempura powder in a bowl, then pour in the egg yolk and mix well. Slowly add water, a little at a time, until the batter has the consistency of sauce. Now add the beer, then mix in the dill and ginger.

Rinse the squid in cold water, then drain and pat dry with a paper towel. Put the squid in a bowl, add the sugar, pepper and salt and shake well to mix.

Fill a heavy-bottomed pan or wok about a third full with oil and place over a medium-high heat. Heat until a little of the batter sizzles on contact with the oil.

Dip the squid rings in the batter, let the excess batter fall away, and then fry the squid in batches for about a minute, until crisp and golden. Remove to a plate lined with a paper towel, to drain.

Serve with the Garlic, Lime and Chilli Dipping Sauce on p.198 and some lemon wedges for squeezing over the calamari.

Vietnamese Coffee with Condensed Milk

When we opened our market café, No.101, in Shoreditch, we inherited an espresso machine and, overnight, we were not just assembling baguettes but also churning out lattes. The shop had a large front window with a long counter which became our favourite spot for watching the world go by. We could hardly tell if we were on the streets of Saigon or Shoreditch.

True Vietnamese coffee uses a slow-drip filter, called a *phin* filter (or use a stove-top espresso-maker for the closest result). The bitter coffee slowly seeps through the steel filter onto a thick layer of creamy condensed milk. To finish, we pour it into another glass with ice cubes and the black and white merge into the distinctive *ca phe* colour of Vietnamese iced coffee.

Makes 1

20ml hot water
20ml condensed milk
A few scoops ground coffee
Ice cubes (optional)

Pour the hot water into a small bowl. Using a cup or glass, pour in the condensed milk. The hot water will 'cook' the condensed milk, but if you like your coffee black, skip the milk.

Grind the coffee fresh, if you have a grinder, or use roast ground coffee, and pack it into the espresso-maker very tightly.

Once the coffee has bubbled into the top of the espresso-maker, add to the condensed milk. Drink hot, or if you prefer iced coffee, pour over ice cubes and enjoy each sip.

Note: if you have a *phin* filter, put it over the cup and fill with ground coffee. Put the top of the *phin* in and press down lightly. Pour in 20ml of boiling water and wait for it to be absorbed. Pour in another 45ml then put the lid on and wait. It's said that a good drip speed is one per second – it should take around 6 minutes.

Vietnamese Yoghurt

Vietnamese yoghurt is smooth, silky and set, with the distinct taste of condensed milk. It's easy to make and a world away from commercial brands. Once you've emptied the can of condensed milk, use the same can to measure out the water, milk and probiotic yoghurt.

Makes 6–8 ramekins

1 x 397g can condensed
  milk
1 can boiling water
2 cans fresh milk
¾ can probiotic yoghurt

Pour the condensed milk into a large bowl. Then fill up the same can with boiling water, swilling it round to scoop up the remaining milk. Pour into the bowl and stir so the milk dissolves completely.

Measure out 2 cans of fresh milk, pour into the bowl and stir again.

Measure out the probiotic yoghurt, pour into the bowl and stir again.

Use a coarse mesh strainer lined with cheesecloth to strain the mixture, twice.

Boil a pan of hot water, to about 70–80°C. If you don't have a thermometer, heat the water until there are small bubbles at the bottom of the pan but don't allow it to boil. Turn off the heat.

Pour the yoghurt mixture into small ramekins or jars. Carefully place these in the pan, so that the water comes two thirds up the sides of the yoghurt jars. Put a lid on the pan, then cover the whole pan in a towel or blanket for 8–10 hours. If it's very cold in your kitchen, change the hot water after 3–4 hours. The finished yoghurt should settle and be very silky, smooth and firm. You can keep one of your pots of yoghurt for the next time so you don't ever have to buy yoghurt again.

To serve, pour over a shot of strong espresso, brewed Vietnamese-style if possible (see p.150).

Note: you can use a yoghurt machine, if you have one, following the manufacturer's instructions.

CHAPTER FIVE

SALTINESS
AND
Healing

The Vietnamese use only one sauce for marinating, cooking, seasoning and eating – and that's fish sauce. Everything else is a derivative of this liquid gold. We use fish sauce as a substitute for salt, and go through a whole bottle every month.

Vietnamese fish sauce is made from fermented anchovies and salt. The best fish sauce is made on Phu Quoc, an island off the coast of Vietnam. Apparently it's the rich coral around the island, which the anchovies feed off, that makes the sauce so good. There are dozens of species of anchovies there, but only the islanders can tell the difference. The sauce is made in giant wooden vats and the higher the protein level the better the sauce. The best fish sauce – virgin pressed like olive oil – has up to 40 nitrogen grams per litre (40N). It should have a dark yet clear amber colour and not contain additives such as MSG, soy or flour.

Good fish sauce has so much flavour, you can pour a spoonful over rice and just eat it like that, in the same way you might dip bread in olive oil. Pick up a bottle from an Asian supermarket or online and start experimenting – it will serve you well.

Everyday Cooking (An Com)

Vietnam has a very long sea coast, and harvesting sea salt is a tradition that has been around for thousands of years. Yet being blessed with this bounty from the sea doesn't mean salt is easy to harvest. In the old days, salt-makers often lost their feet from standing in the saline water for too long. And, even today, during the monsoon season, rain can suddenly descend on a field of harvested salt, melting it into water again, and wiping out a day's work in a blink.

Salt is, of course, part of everyday cooking. In Vietnam there are no fewer than 20 types: 'live' salt fresh from the salt field; roasted salt; powdered salt; stewed salt; salt and pepper; salt and chilli; salt and lemongrass; salt and galangal; salt and prawns; salt and peanuts; salt and sesame; salt and garlic; and so on. In Hue there's a traditional meal called *com muoi*, which literally means rice and salt. It sounds so simple, it could be taken for peasant fare. But it's actually an elaborate feast reserved for special occasions – where the rice is served with more than ten kinds of flavoured salt – to be shared only with close friends or lovers.

Chargrilled Salmon with Ginger, Black Pepper and Fish Sauce

On our first trip to the island of Phu Quoc, we headed south and stopped by a food stall on the beach. The stall belonged to a young woman, whose dog was running around on the beach while her son slept peacefully in a hammock. She served us the most delectable grilled fish, marinated in the island's own fish sauce. The fish tasted so fresh – it had come straight from the sea. Here, we've recreated the dish from memory, and added a kick of ginger and black pepper to balance the salty marinade.

Serves 2

200g salmon fillet, cut into
  2 pieces

Marinade:
25g piece fresh ginger,
  peeled and thinly sliced
1 tbsp fish sauce
½ tsp sugar
1 tsp fresh lemon juice
1 tsp freshly ground black
  pepper
1 tsp crushed garlic

To garnish:
1 tbsp chopped spring onion
1 tbsp chopped fresh dill

Combine the marinade ingredients in a bowl, add the salmon and use a pastry brush to spread the marinade evenly over the salmon. Cover and leave in the fridge for 30 minutes.

If you are outdoors, cook the salmon on a charcoal grill (or gas barbecue) for about 7 minutes on each side, or you can cook in a preheated oven at 200°C/gas 6 for 8–12 minutes.

Scatter the spring onion and chopped dill over the salmon before serving.

Shoulder of Lamb with Vietnamese Miso

Soya bean paste, made from fermented soya beans, is widely used across Asia. The Japanese have their *miso*, the Koreans have their *ssamjang*, and the Vietnamese have their *tuong ban*. This marinade has an intense flavour and is one of Anh's more experimental recipes. For best results, try to source an authentic Vietnamese soya bean paste in an Asian supermarket or online.

Serves 6

1kg shoulder of lamb,
  off the bone
2 tbsp vodka
1 tbsp finely chopped fresh
  ginger

Marinade:
5 tbsp soya bean paste
1 tbsp finely chopped
  galangal (or ginger)
1 tbsp crushed garlic
½ tbsp five spice powder
1 tbsp fresh pear juice
1 tbsp finely chopped
  shallot
3 tbsp sesame oil
1 tbsp ground black
  pepper
½ tbsp chilli powder or
  ground paprika

Cut the lamb into strips about 2cm thick.

In a bowl, mix the vodka with the ginger and rub into the lamb strips. Then rinse the meat under cold running water and pat dry with paper towels. This cleans the lamb and helps to remove the lamb's odour.

Combine the marinade ingredients in a large bowl or dish. Add the lamb, then cover and leave in the fridge for an hour, or ideally overnight.

When ready to cook, thread the lamb pieces onto skewers, spreading them evenly along each skewer.

Cook under a hot grill for 10 minutes on each side, or until done. You can also barbecue over a medium-hot charcoal grill or gas barbecue.

Chargrilled Sea Bass

Serves 4

1 whole sea bass (about 500g)

Marinade:
1 garlic clove, chopped
1 bird's-eye chilli, finely chopped
50g piece fresh ginger, peeled and roughly chopped
2–4 sprigs fresh dill, chopped
1 tbsp sugar
4 tbsp fresh lemon juice
4 tbsp water
2 tbsp fish sauce, or to taste
1–2 lemongrass sticks, lightly crushed

Another take on chargrilled fish. Here, the dill takes the dish in a whole new direction.

Scale and clean the fish.

To make the marinade, combine the garlic, chilli, ginger, dill, sugar and lemon juice with the water. Add the fish sauce.

Using the point of a sharp knife, make 3 slits through the skin of the fish on each side. Pour a few teaspoons of the marinade inside the fish and tuck in the lemongrass, then rub the remainder of the marinade all over the skin. Cover and leave to marinate for 20–30 minutes.

Cook under a hot grill for 10 minutes on each side, or until thoroughly cooked. You can also barbecue over a medium-hot charcoal grill or gas barbecue.

Serve with potatoes and a simple salad for a stunning-looking main course. Or strip off flakes of fish to put inside summer rolls (see p.171).

Photo overleaf

Asparagus and Sprouting Broccoli with Peanuts and Black Sesame Salt

The sea salt, ground peanut and sesame seed mix used here makes a simple but magical seasoning that can be used in a variety of dishes. In our schooldays, sometimes our packed lunch would simply be rice, pressed into dumplings and then dipped in this peanut and sesame mix.

Serves 4

200g asparagus tips
200g purple-sprouting
   broccoli

Seasoning:
2 tbsp salted roasted
   peanuts
1 tbsp sea salt
1 tbsp sesame seeds

Shallot butter:
5g butter
2 tbsp dried shallots
   (or toasted dried onion)

Crush the roasted peanuts with the sea salt in a pestle and mortar (or use a grinder or food processor). Add the sesame seeds and pound again, then mix well.

Put a frying pan over a medium heat and add the butter.

Add the dried shallots and toss for a couple of minutes until golden, crispy and fragrant. Pour this shallot butter into a jug or bowl.

Add the asparagus and the sprouting broccoli to the same frying pan and stir-fry them for a couple of minutes – they will cook faster if you put a lid on the pan.

Remove the asparagus and sprouting broccoli to a serving plate. Drizzle the shallot butter and sprinkle the peanut and sesame salt mixture over the vegetables, and serve.

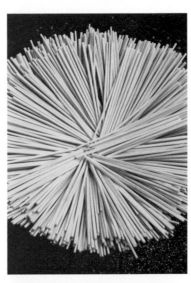

Festive Cooking
(An Qua)

In this section we've included a *banh mi* baguette recipe which we call Fish Q. The inspiration for this came from a cult dish that you could find in only one restaurant in the Old Quarter of Hanoi: fish cooked in hot oil at your table. We only ate there when my father had special visitors in town, and that dish was one of the true treats of my childhood. I described the taste to Anh and, before I knew it, Fish Q was on our menu even though she hadn't even tasted the original dish. This is typical of the way we operate – we imagine how a dish tastes when we might only have read about it, or seen a picture, or literally dreamt it. And then we experiment in the kitchen, tasting our way until we hit the right notes. There are parts of Vietnam we've never explored and dishes we've never tasted, so our cooking is not just about replication, but imagination.

Intuition and versatility are always useful in cooking, but for us they are indispensable, because we are taking an age-old ethnic cuisine and attempting to make it work in modern kitchens.

Hanoi Prawn Fritters *(Banh Tom)*

This is our reinterpretation of a dish familiar to anyone from Hanoi, the prawn fritter of West Lake. West Lake is like a village made up only of restaurants, and its visitors are on a food-pilgrimage.

Makes 12 fritters

1 or 2 sweet potatoes,
    about 300g total
500g fresh prawns, peeled
200ml vegetable oil
1 garlic clove, sliced
¼ green papaya (optional)
1 carrot
2 tsp salt
1 tsp sugar
2 tsp rice vinegar

Batter:
2 egg yolks
200g plain flour
100g rice flour
1 tsp sugar
2 tbsp water
½ tsp salt
½ tsp gia vi (or a mix of
    2 parts sugar, 1 part
    sea salt, 1 part ground
    black pepper, 1 part
    garlic powder)

Peel the sweet potatoes and shred into long strips, using a grater or food processor.

To make the batter, mix the egg yolks with the flours and the sugar. Add the water, salt and gia vi.

Add the potato strips to the batter. Cover and leave in the fridge for 30 minutes.

Combine the marinade ingredients in a bowl, add the prawns and leave for 20 minutes.

Heat the oil in a frying pan, throw in the sliced garlic and stir quickly until the oil is fragrant.

Add the prawns and cook for a couple of minutes until they turn red. Don't overcook the prawns since they'll be fried once more.

Roughly line up a single 5cm-long layer of potato strips on a metal slotted spoon or spatula. Using the same frying pan, lower into the oil for a couple of minutes until golden. Lift out of the oil and lay a couple of prawns on top of the potato strips, then submerge in the oil again. Remove to a plate lined with paper towels. Now fry another single layer of potato strips and sandwich this on top of the prawns. It should now look like a prawn toast, using sweet potato for the sandwich.

Now repeat the process and you should have roughly 12 fritters in total.

Marinade:
1 tsp crushed garlic
1 tsp freshly ground pepper
1 tsp gia vi (or a mix of
  2 parts sugar, 1 part
  sea salt, 1 part ground
  black pepper, 1 part
  garlic powder)
1 tbsp fish sauce
½ tsp sugar

To serve:
Garlic, Lime and Chilli
  Dipping Sauce (see p. 198)
1 round lettuce
A few sprigs mint
A few sprigs coriander
A few sprigs basil

Shred the papaya (if using) and carrot into thin slithers, using a grater or food processor, and soak in cold water with 1 tsp of salt for 10 minutes. Drain the papaya and carrot and leave to dry.

Put the shredded papaya and carrot into a mixing bowl. Add the remaining teaspoon of salt and squeeze the shredded papaya and carrot with your hands. Add the sugar and the rice vinegar. This will lightly pickle the vegetables.

Make up the dipping sauce on p.198 and add the pickled vegetables.

Wrap each fritter in a lettuce leaf with a little mint, coriander and basil and serve alongside the vegetable dip.

Note: green papaya is a special variety found in Asian supermarkets. Don't use yellow papaya as it will disintegrate.

Prawn Summer Rolls

Summer rolls are amazingly fresh and delicious. I'd like to think that in ten years, they will be as widely available as sushi is now. The basics you will need are rice paper wraps, fresh herbs and a pinch of vermicelli noodles. On top of that you can experiment with pretty much any fillings. The dipping sauces are equally imaginative, from peanut sauce to garlic and lime. It's a gorgeous way to pack so many fresh flavours in one bite. Rolling them can be tricky at first, but after a couple of goes you'll crack it. Children are good at making summer rolls! This recipe makes a fun family activity, rolling and eating at the table together.

Makes 10 summer rolls

100ml coconut milk
1 lemongrass stick
  (optional)
10–15 cooked peeled large
  prawns

To assemble summer rolls:
10 sheets rice paper
100g rice vermicelli noodles,
  cooked according to
  packet instructions
1 round lettuce

200g carrots, shredded
1 cucumber, cut into
  matchsticks
½ pineapple, cut into
  matchsticks
1 bunch coriander

To serve:
Garlic, Lime and Chilli
  Dipping Sauce (see p.198)

Heat the coconut milk, add the lemongrass stick (if using) and the prawns and cook for 2–3 minutes. Discard the lemongrass, drain the prawns and set to one side.

For the summer rolls, lay the sheets of rice paper on a chopping board. Put a bowl of cold water next to it and, with wet fingers, pat the rice papers until they are moist and pliable, but not too wet or they will tear.

Place a pinch of cooked noodles on the centre of one sheet. Add a leaf of lettuce. Add a pinch of shredded carrot and a stick of cucumber and pineapple.

Fold the rice paper over once.

Cut the prawns in half and place neatly on the rice paper with a sprig of coriander.

Fold the two sides of the rice paper in and roll up the whole length of the paper.

Repeat until you are out of fillings.

Make up the Garlic, Lime and Chilli Dipping Sauce on p.198.

Serve the summer rolls with the dipping sauce.

Note: you can make summer rolls with any other meat or fish instead of prawns. Using this recipe, you could also add chive and thin slices of boiled pork belly for a classic Saigon street-food version. Our favourite filling for a family feast is the Chargrilled Sea Bass from p.161.

Making Summer/Spring Rolls:

After experimenting with several types of rice paper for summer rolls, we finally figured out that the simplest way to prepare the rice paper is to submerge it in boiling hot water before rolling. This makes it very soft and easy to work with, and the water evaporates quickly so that the rice paper is not soaked.

Put less filling on the rice paper than you think you'll need, then roll almost to the end of the paper, fold in the sides and roll over again.

We wrap our summer rolls in round lettuce leaves before eating them so they retain their moisture.

You can use this same technique with rice paper for spring rolls, but wrap the rice paper in lettuce leaves the night before you want to roll them. In Vietnam we use banana leaves, but any type of leafy vegetable should do the trick. This gives the rice paper just enough moisture to make it easier to work with, but not so much that it disintegrates as you roll.

Pork Nem Spring Rolls

Nem, as we call a spring roll in the north of Vietnam, is the food served at family feasts like weddings and anniversaries. Eating *nem* is one of our earliest childhood memories and it reminds us of the excitement of large family get-togethers. This recipe is how our mothers taught us to make it, although we never seem to get the rolls as perfectly crispy as them!

Makes 20 rolls

Filling:
2 carrots
50g dried shiitake
  mushrooms
50g dried wood ear
  mushrooms (or use
  another 50g shiitake)
100g glass noodles
300g pork mince
1 tsp freshly ground pepper
1 tbsp fish sauce
100g white crabmeat
1 tsp finely chopped shallot
1 tsp finely chopped garlic
3–4 tsp chopped spring
  onion
2 eggs

Assembling and frying:
1 tbsp vinegar
100ml water
20 sheets rice paper
Vegetable oil for frying

To serve:
Garlic, Lime and Chilli
  Dipping Sauce (see p.198)

Wash and peel the carrots. Shred the carrots into long slithers, using a grater.

Soak the shiitake and wood ear mushrooms in hot water for about 15 minutes. Drain and pat dry with a paper towel, then slice thinly.

Soak the glass noodles in cold water for about 15 minutes, then drain and cut into 5cm lengths.

In a mixing bowl, mix the pork with the pepper and fish sauce. Stir in the crabmeat, working it well into the mixture. Add the mushrooms and noodles. Add the carrot together with the shallot, garlic and spring onion. Crack 2 eggs into the mixture, and stir well. Set aside until you are ready to assemble the rolls.

When you are ready to roll, mix together the vinegar and water in a small bowl. Brush a little of this on the rice papers before rolling them, to soften them slightly and make them more malleable.

Take one sheet of rice paper at a time. When rolling, our mothers' trick is to first fold over the rice paper once, then put the filling on the folded part. Now roll twice almost to the end of the rice paper, then fold the 2 sides in and roll again. Brush on some of the vinegar and water to seal the fold. Repeat with the remaining sheets and filling.

Heat a generous amount of oil in a small, heavy-bottomed pan or deep frying pan. When the oil is hot, gently add the *nem*, one at a time, turning them once in the oil to make sure they are coated. Carefully remove to a plate lined with paper towels, to drain.

Make up the Garlic, Lime and Chilli Dipping Sauce on p.198. The sauce is best served warm – to do this, microwave it lightly before serving. Serve the *nem* with the dipping sauce.

Fish Nem Spring Rolls

We came up with this dish for our pop-up supper clubs. To accommodate an array of food allergies and dietary requirements, we made almost all the menu seafood. *Nem* is traditionally made with minced pork but we like using sea bass too for its texture, although you could substitute with any other firm fish. This recipe nods to the past while experimenting in the present.

Makes 15–20 rolls

Filling:
300g sea bass fillet
1 tsp crushed garlic
2 tsp grated fresh ginger
2 tbsp chopped fresh dill
1 tsp freshly ground pepper
1 tbsp fish sauce
1 carrot

Assembling and frying:
1 tbsp vinegar
100ml water
15–20 sheets rice paper
Vegetable oil for frying

To serve:
Ginger and Dill Dipping Sauce (see p.200)

Use a food processor to mince the sea bass fillet until it forms an elastic paste. Mix in the garlic, ginger and dill, then add the ground pepper and fish sauce. Grate the carrot and add to the mix. Set aside until you are ready to assemble the rolls.

When you are ready to roll, mix together the vinegar and water in a small bowl. Brush a little of this on the rice papers before rolling them, to soften them slightly and make them more malleable.

Take one sheet of rice paper at a time. First fold over the rice paper once, then put a little of the filling on the folded part. Now roll twice almost to the end of the rice paper, then fold the 2 sides in and roll again. Brush on some of the vinegar and water to seal the fold. Repeat with the remaining sheets and filling.

Heat a generous amount of oil in a small, heavy-bottomed pan or deep frying pan. When the oil is hot, gently add the *nem*, one at a time, turning them once in the oil to make sure they are coated. Carefully remove to a plate lined with paper towels, to drain.

Make up the Ginger and Dill Dipping Sauce on p.200. The sauce is best served warm – to do this, microwave it lightly before serving.

Serve the *nem* with the dipping sauce.

Note: the key to making *nem* crispy is to ensure that all the ingredients are dry. It's therefore a good idea to prepare the filling in advance and let it air-dry in a colander before rolling and frying the *nem* just before serving.

Prawn Summer Rolls in Sweetheart Cabbage

The traditional recipe uses mustard greens for a tangy and fresh taste. However, as these are not readily available in UK supermarkets, we've substituted it with sweetheart cabbage, or you could equally well use Chinese leaf.

Serves 4

1 sweetheart (pointed)
    cabbage, about 6–7cm
    in length
200g lean pork belly
Pinch of salt
20g sliced fresh ginger
100ml coconut milk
20g chopped lemongrass
200g peeled fresh prawns
1 egg
1 tbsp vegetable oil
150g Vietnamese pork ham
    (optional)
1–2 bunches chives or
    spring onions
½ pack rice vermicelli
    noodles

To serve:
Peanut Sauce (see p.200)

Cut the cabbage in half, remove and discard the hard core and separate the leaves. Boil the leaves for about 5 minutes in a large pan, then soak in cold water for about 2 minutes. Drain and leave to dry.

Bring water to boil in a large pan (you can use the same pan), then boil the pork belly with a pinch of salt and the slices of ginger for about 30 minutes. Remove the pork to a chopping board, pat dry and then cut into slices about 1cm in width.

Wash out the pan, then pour in the coconut milk, add the lemongrass and bring to the boil. Add the prawns and cook until they turn red. Immediately drain the prawns in a colander, then rinse quickly under cold water and leave to dry.

Whisk the egg. Heat the oil in a frying pan, then add the egg and make a very thin omelette (like a pancake). Then slice the egg into long, thin strips.

Prepare the pork ham (if using) by slicing it into long, thin strips.

Cut the chives or spring onions into 10cm lengths and blanch in hot water for 2–3 minutes.

Cook the rice noodles according to the packet instructions, then drain and leave to dry.

To assemble the rolls, lay a cabbage leaf flat on a chopping board and put a teaspoonful of rice noodles on it. Top with 1–2 prawns and a couple of slices of omelette, pork ham and pork belly. Then roll up the cabbage leaf and tie with a length of chive or spring onion. Use scissors to trim the ends of the roll. Repeat with the remaining cabbage leaves and filling.

Serve the rolls with the Peanut Sauce on p.200.

Fish Q Vietnamese Baguette *(Banh Mi)*

We tested endless recipes for a fish *banh mi*, before I finally thought of the dish from the restaurant my father took me to as a childhood treat: fish cooked at the table in hot oil. The pungent marinade on that fish was an acquired taste. It was also out of the reach of my father's pockets most of the time, as it was one of the most expensive meals in Hanoi's Old Quarter then. But I never forgot it.

For the recipe here, we finally cracked the marinade, then introduced red onion and peanuts for a *banh mi*-style crunch to complement the delicate fish.

Cut the fish fillet into 2cm cubes.

To prepare the marinade, put the oil in a frying pan over a medium heat. When hot, add the shallots, garlic and galangal (or ginger). Toss until fragrant, then transfer to a bowl.

In a separate bowl, add the shrimp paste and slowly stir in the lemon juice, mixing well in a circular motion. You should see some small white bubbles as you mix them together. Add the sugar and let it rest for a moment.

Take the bowl of shallots, garlic and ginger, and mix in the gia vi and fish sauce, then add the shrimp paste mixture and mix well. Finally, add the turmeric and yoghurt and stir again.

Add the fish cubes to this marinade and massage the fish so that it absorbs the marinade. Cover with clingfilm and put in the fridge for a couple of hours.

When ready to cook, grill the marinated fish over medium-hot coals on a charcoal grill (or use a gas barbecue) or cook under a hot grill for 10 minutes on each side, or until thoroughly cooked.

Put the oil into a frying pan over a medium-high heat. When the oil is hot, add the dill and spring onion and toss until they are softened but still green. Now add the cooked fish in batches and toss again. You can add extra oil if needed.

Serves 2

200g firm white fish
   (sea bass, whiting, cod,
   or catfish), deboned
   and skinned
3 tbsp vegetable oil
1 bunch dill, chopped
½ spring onion, chopped

Marinade:
2 tbsp vegetable oil
1 tbsp finely chopped
   shallots
1 tbsp crushed garlic
1 tbsp finely chopped fresh
   galangal (or ginger)
½ tbsp shrimp paste
1 tbsp fresh lemon juice
1 tbsp sugar
½ tbsp gia vi (or a mix of
   2 parts sugar, 1 part
   sea salt, 1 part ground
   black pepper, 1 part
   garlic powder)
1 tbsp fish sauce
1 tbsp ground turmeric
½ tbsp yoghurt

To assemble the banh mi:
1 baguette, about 20cm long
½ tbsp mayo
Carrot and Daikon Pickle,
* to taste (see p. 196)*
Red Onion Pickle, to taste
* (see p. 195)*
5 slices cucumber
A couple of fresh coriander
* sprigs*

To garnish:
1 tbsp crushed salted
* peanuts*
Chopped fresh chillies
* or chilli sauce, to taste*

To assemble the banh mi:
Slice the baguette lengthways on the diagonal. Spread the mayo evenly on both sides.

Spread Carrot and Daikon Pickle and Red Onion Pickle to taste along the bread.

Add the fish with the dill and spring onion.

Add the cucumber and coriander sprigs.

Sprinkle some crushed peanuts over, to finish. If you wish, you can add chopped fresh chillies or chilli sauce, to taste.

Photo overleaf

Social Cooking
(An Choi)

A salty flavour lends itself perfectly to small plates, like the salads and snacks included here. Simple to execute and effective, what's not to like about a sea bass carpaccio or a chicory and tofu salad.

Chicory and Tofu Salad with Sesame, Soy and Ginger Dressing

This is one of the most fabulous salads we have 'cooked', although cooking is an overstatement because it's beyond simple to put together.

Serves 2

200g soft tofu
1 head of chicory
1 pomegranate
1 pack salad cress

Dressing:
2 tbsp sugar
4 tbsp warm water
4 tbsp soy sauce
1 tsp grated fresh ginger
1 tbsp sesame oil
Juice of 1 clementine

Cut the tofu into 1–2cm cubes, about the same size as sugar cubes.

Separate the chicory leaves and wash them.

Cut the pomegranate in half and remove the seeds.

For the dressing, put the sugar and water in a heavy-bottomed pan over a medium heat until the sugar has completely dissolved. Stir in the soy sauce, grated ginger and sesame oil. Cut the clementine in half and squeeze the juice into the pan.

Arrange the chicory leaves in a flower petal configuration on a plate. Spoon the tofu cubes over the leaves, sprinkle the salad cress on top, then drizzle the dressing over and top with the pomegranate seeds.

Sea Bass Carpaccio

I've always thought Italian and Vietnamese food have much in common. Both countries are long and boot-shaped, with diverse regional cuisines and a big appetite for food. This is one of the most obvious examples of how the two styles cross over.

Serves 4

1 sea bass fillet (about
300g), skinned
2 tbsp fresh lime juice
A few coriander leaves,
to garnish

Shallot oil:
2 tbsp vegetable oil
1 tbsp dried shallots
(or toasted dried onions)

To serve:
Ginger and Dill Dipping
Sauce (see p.200)

Cut the sea bass fillet in half lengthways and then cut into thin slices. This is easy to do if you part-freeze it first (see p.209).

Place the sea bass slices on a plate in a single layer and drizzle the lime juice over them. Set aside.

To make the shallot oil, put the vegetable oil in a frying pan over a medium heat. When the oil is hot, add the dried shallots and toss for about 1–2 minutes until golden and crispy. Carefully pour this shallot oil into a heatproof bowl and set aside

Make the Ginger and Dill Dipping Sauce on p.200.

Add the sea bass slices to the dipping sauce and leave for about 1 minute, then remove to a plate, arranging the slices in a single layer.

Drizzle some shallot oil over the carpaccio and garnish with coriander leaves.

Fresh Prawns Steamed in Beer with Chilli Lime Salt Pepper

Serves 4

A quick recipe that's perfect with a glass of cold beer.

1 x 250ml bottle of beer
1 bunch fresh lemongrass
1kg fresh prawns, unpeeled
Pinch of sea salt

Dipping sauce:
3 tbsp coarse sea salt
2 tbsp freshly ground black pepper
Juice of 1–2 limes
3 tsp finely chopped bird's-eye chillies, or to taste

Reserve a tablespoon of the beer, then pour the rest into the bottom of a pan and bring to the boil.

Using a rolling pin or the broad side of a knife, crush the lemongrass stalks.

Lay the crushed lemongrass in a steamer basket or metal colander and sit it above the pan. Arrange the prawns on top of the lemongrass.

Sprinkle a pinch of sea salt and the reserved beer over the prawns, and steam for around 5–7 minutes, or until the prawns turn red.

Tip the prawns into a serving bowl and discard the lemongrass.

To make the dipping sauce, mix the sea salt and ground pepper in a bowl. Squeeze the lime juice into the bowl and mix well. Finally, add chopped chilli to taste. You are ready to start peeling, dipping and eating your prawns.

Baked Sweet Potato with Peanut Crème Fraîche

Serves 1

1 sweet potato
2 tbsp crème fraîche
1 tbsp ground peanuts

Sweet potato and corn on the cob are the favourite late-night snacks in Vietnam. Around ten o'clock, street vendors peddle their bicycles around the neighbourhoods and shout out their wares. There the sweet potato is nibbled on its own, but here we've souped it up with crème fraîche and salty peanuts. You could also chargrill the sweet potato instead of baking, perfect for a summer evening in the back garden.

Preheat the oven to 200°C/gas 6.

Cut the sweet potato in half, wrap in foil and bake in the oven for about 45 minutes or until soft.

Mix the crème fraîche with the peanuts and spoon over the potato halves.

Sweetcorn with Sesame Butter

This light snack is also inspired by the cobs served by pedlars bicycling through the empty streets of late-night Vietnam. We've brightened it with a spoon of butter and sprinkling of sesame seeds. Pick up a couple of cobs from the market in autumn, when they are freshly harvested and full of flavour.

Serves 1

1 cob sweetcorn, husk
   removed
5g butter, softened
A few sesame seeds

Preheat the oven to 180°C/gas 4.

Put the sweetcorn on a greased baking sheet or in a baking dish. Use a brush to spread the butter over the sweetcorn. Bake in the oven for 15 minutes.

When the sweetcorn is cooked, sprinkle the sesame seeds on top.

When we set up our very first stall on Broadway Market in 2009, we had no idea what path it would lead us down or how much it would change the way we eat and live. Like many in our generation, we were lost in making a living, while never quite feeling we had a life. We followed recipes for success that were cooked up by others – until we decided to take life into our own hands. We never trained as chefs, the only food education we had was our own hunger, but we were young and hungry to taste the world. It's still too early to say whether Banhmi11 will succeed, at least by the measures of the city analysts that we once were. But one thing is for sure, for us the ingredients for happiness are simple: a purpose, a passion and, in cooking, a palate that can be cultivated with time and training. Banhmi11 has given us food, 'family' and a way of life. And for these reasons alone, we would never look back.

VIETNAMESE
— *Kitchen* —
ESSENTIALS

MASTER RECIPES

Annatto Seed Oil

Makes 100ml

100ml vegetable oil
10g annatto seeds

Annatto seed oil adds colour and fragrance to a dish, while remaining neutral in taste.

Heat the oil in a frying pan. Throw in an annatto seed and if it sizzles and makes bubbles, the oil is hot enough. Now you can add the remaining annatto seeds. Cook for 2–3 minutes, stirring constantly so the seeds don't burn.

Turn off the heat and let the oil cool a little. Then carefully strain the oil through a fine mesh sieve and discard the seeds. You will have an orange-coloured oil with fragrance from the annatto seeds.

This will store in a jar for 2 months.

Broth

Broth is a cornerstone of Vietnamese cooking because it is the basis of noodle soups. Homemade broth takes a long time but it is worth it! Once you have created a flavoursome stock you have laid the foundation for an amazing meal. Whatever you then do with that broth is really just a form of garnishing. Broth is the Vietnamese equivalent of European stock and, as with stock, you can strain and freeze broth. We often just leave the bones in the bottom of the stockpot though, and make sure not to ladle them when we pour out bowls of noodle soup. If you want to make broth in bulk just double up all the ingredients listed.

Makes about 2 litres

4l water
2kg beef bones, cleansed
200g fresh ginger, peeled and sliced
2 tbsp salt

Beef Broth

Cleansing beef bones:
To cleanse beef bones, bring 2l of water to boil in a stockpot, add ½ tbsp of salt and 50g of sliced ginger.

When the water is boiled, add the beef bones, reduce to a medium heat and bring to the boil again.

After about 5 minutes, remove the bones and rinse under cold water.

Use a small, sharp knife to remove any residual meat or muscles and take out the bone marrow, and discard.

Then soak the bones in cold water with ½ tbsp of salt and 50g of sliced ginger.

To make broth:

In a large stockpot, bring 2l of water to a boil and add 100g of ginger and 1 tbsp of salt.

Once the water is boiled, add the cleansed beef bones and reduce the heat until the water's at an almost imperceptible simmer. You should see tiny bubbles. Watch the pot carefully as if the heat is too high, the stock will be cloudy.

Cook for as long as you can, at least 4 hours. As the broth reduces, top up with more hot water to the same level as when you started out.

Once done, you can transfer the stock to a large container and store in the fridge; it will keep for 5 days. You can also freeze for later use.

Chicken Broth

Makes about 2 litres

2l water
1 chicken carcass or 300g
  chicken bones
100g sliced ginger
2 tbsp salt

To clean the chicken carcass, first rinse it under cold running water. Then rub 1 tbsp of salt into the carcass and rinse again.

In a stockpot, bring 2l of water to a boil and add the sliced ginger and 1 tbsp of salt. Once boiled, put the chicken carcass in, ensuring there's enough water to submerge the carcass and cover about 3cm above.

Reduce the heat to low, leave the pot uncovered, and boil for an hour. Use a spoon to gently scoop out any foam or fat that surfaces, keeping the stock clear.

Vegetable Broth

Makes about 2 litres

2l water
2 carrots
1 celeriac
1 swede
½ daikon radish (optional)
1 tsp salt

Wash and peel the vegetables, then cut them into large chunks.

In a stockpot, bring 2l of water to a boil and add the salt. Once boiling, add the vegetable chunks, ensuring there's enough water to submerge the vegetables.

Once boiling again, reduce the heat and cook for 45 minutes to an hour.

The longer you cook the vegetables, the sweeter the broth will taste.

Caramel Water

Caramel is a fundamental ingredient in clay pot cooking and grilling, and adds a concentrated, but not saccharine sweetness to marinades. Melting the sugar removes water and brings out the flavours. This caramel water has a more liquid consistency than the caramel sauce used for braising.

Makes about 250ml

50g sugar
250ml hot water

Place a heavy-bottomed pan over a medium heat. Make sure there's no water residue in the pan before you add the sugar – if necessary, wipe out the pan with a paper towel (it's best to wear oven gloves to do this).

Add the sugar to the pan and keep over a medium heat, without stirring, for 2–3 minutes. You can shake the pan slightly so the sugar spreads out and melts evenly.

Once the sugar starts to foam and turn brown, lower the heat and stir constantly with a wooden spoon, to ensure there is no burned sugar at the bottom. The sugar will become pale amber or golden brown in colour. Pour in the hot water and stir again.

Cook until the caramel starts to boil, then remove from the heat.

You can store it for a week in the fridge.

Note: hot water helps the sugar to caramelise faster and results in a more pronounced flavour. There will inevitably be some foaming as the caramel boils so be careful. It's best not to let the caramel get too dark and to err on the lighter brown side before pouring in the water, otherwise the sugar will burn very quickly and build up steam in minutes.

Pickle Brine

Makes about 200ml

2 tbsp sugar
1 tbsp gia vi (or a mix of 2 parts sugar, 1 part sea salt, 1 part ground black pepper, 1 part garlic powder)
100ml lukewarm water
100ml lemon juice

When we started making carrot and daikon pickle for *banh mi*, we tried various techniques for making pickling brine and discovered that it doesn't have to be complicated. We stopped using vinegar, because it was hard to find natural rice vinegar from fermented rice, not chemicals, and the pickles in vinegar brine came out stark and sour. So we prefer to use lemon juice. Lemons have a clear, crisp and mild sourness and preserve vegetables beautifully. The sourness from vinegar is more acidic, and can be very sharp, so if you prefer to use vinegar you may want to add more sugar to balance out the sourness.

Dissolve the sugar and gia vi in the lukewarm water. Add the lemon juice and mix well.

Red Onion Pickle

Makes about 500–700g

500g red onions
1l hot water
200ml Pickle Brine (see above)

We use this pickle as an accompaniment to our Fish Q *banh mi* on our market stall, and it always attracts a lot of attention. It's also great with fish and grilled meat.

Slice the red onions. Pour the hot water over the onions, then leave for a few minutes before draining them.

Pour the pickle brine over the onions.

Transfer to a food container, or sterilised jars, making sure the onions are fully submerged in the brine. Leave in the fridge overnight.

The pickle will keep for up to 2 weeks in the fridge.

To serve, squeeze out any residual brine.

Carrot and Daikon Pickle

Makes about 500–700g

500g carrots
200g daikon radish
  (or substitute with carrot)
1l hot water
1 tsp salt
200ml Pickle Brine
  (see p. 195)

Wash and peel the carrots and daikon radish. Use a grater or vegetable peeler to shave off thin strips, or cut them into sticks about 5cm long and 2cm thick.

Pour the hot water into a pan, add the salt and bring to the boil.

Pour the water over the carrot and daikon, and let them sit for 3–5 minutes. This will soften and slightly cook the vegetables, so they will last longer and absorb the brine better. You don't want them too soft, though, and they should still be crunchy when you drain them.

Drain the vegetables and transfer to a mixing bowl. Add the pickle brine, and mix well.

Transfer to food containers, or sterilised jars, making sure the carrot and daikon are fully submerged in the brine. Leave in the fridge overnight.

The pickle will keep for up to 2 weeks in the fridge in a sterilised jar.

To serve, squeeze out any residual brine.

Note: daikon radish – also known as mooli – is available in many supermarkets, in oriental shops or Indian or Turkish greengrocers.

To sterilise jars, wash them thoroughly in warm soapy water, then rinse in clean warm water. Allow them to drip-dry, upside down, on a rack in a medium oven for 5 minutes.

SAUCES

Dipping Sauce *(Nuoc Cham)*

Nuoc is water, and *cham* means to dip, and *nuoc cham* literally means dipping sauce.

If we had to pick one dish to epitomise this cookbook, it would have to be *nuoc cham*. Here is the union of sweet, sour, spicy, bitter and salty, and the dominance or mildness of any one flavour is dependent on the dish it accompanies.

Nuoc cham is a complex combination of flavours, and if you don't get it right first time, it's very difficult to distinguish what to adjust, whether to add more sugar, lemon juice, fish sauce or just water. In Vietnam, *nuoc cham* is usually prepared in consultation with other family members, and it's a compliment to your palate to be asked.

Some people chop the garlic and chillies, while others grind them using a pestle and mortar or press them using the broad side of a knife. We use a food processor to chop them finely and always have a small box stored in the fridge, where they keep for a couple of days. Whichever way you choose, be sure to taste after adding each ingredient.

There are endless variations on *nuoc cham*. At Banhmi11 we add finely chopped pineapple to give it a sweet note.

We also add ginger and dill to dipping sauce to serve with fish, and tamarind to eat with summer rolls. Some recipes are spicier, some are sourer, some are dark and concentrated like a sauce, and some are light like a dressing.

Garlic, Lime and Chilli Dipping Sauce

Serves 4

2 tbsp sugar
6 tbsp warm water
4 tbsp lime juice
2 tbsp crushed garlic
4 tbsp fish sauce
1 tsp chopped bird's-eye
  chilli
Freshly ground black
  pepper, to taste

Dissolve the sugar in the warm water.

Once the sugar has completely dissolved, add the lime juice. Taste as you go to ensure that the dressing is to your liking. At this point, it should taste like really good lemonade.

Add the garlic and stir well.

Gradually stir in the fish sauce, adding just enough to suit your taste. This way you can control its pungency.

Add the chopped chilli and then grind over some fresh pepper, to taste.

Ginger and Dill Dipping Sauce

Serves 4

1 tbsp sugar
4 tbsp warm water
1 tbsp lime juice
1 tsp chopped garlic
1 tbsp fish sauce
2 tsp finely chopped fresh
   ginger
2 tbsp chopped fresh dill
Chopped chillies, to taste
Freshly ground black
   pepper, to taste

Dissolve the sugar in the warm water.

Once the sugar has completely dissolved, stir in the lime juice.

Add the garlic and stir well.

Gradually stir in the fish sauce, adding just enough to suit your taste.

Add the ginger and stir well.

Stir in the chopped dill.

Add the chopped chilli and then grind over some fresh pepper, to taste.

Peanut Sauce

Serves 4

1 tbsp glutinous rice
   powder
50ml cold water
1 tsp vegetable oil
½ tsp crushed garlic
200g crushed peanuts
1 tsp fish sauce
1 tsp salt
1 tbsp sugar
2–3 tbsp hot water
1 tbsp white wine

Mix the glutinous rice powder with the cold water so the powder dissolves in the water completely.

Heat the oil in a heavy-bottomed pan, add the garlic and toss until the oil becomes fragrant. Add the peanuts and toss in the garlic oil for a couple of minutes until the liquid becomes fragrant.

Now pour the rice powder water into the peanuts and stir in a circular motion for a couple of minutes to combine the sauce well.

In a bowl, mix the fish sauce, salt and sugar into the hot water, then add to the sauce and stir again.

Using a hand blender, blend the sauce so that everything is well combined.

Stir the white wine into the sauce, to finish.

Tamarind Sauce

Apart from Prawn Tamarind on p.73, we haven't given another specific recipe to use this dipping sauce with. But we've included it here because it's great as a condiment for grilled fish and shellfish. You can find tamarind in oriental food shops or online. It's frequently used in Indian, Chinese, Thai and Vietnamese cooking. Use the pulp which comes in plastic wrapped slabs, not the paste that comes in jars, and cut out a fraction of the slab, as if slicing fudge.

Serves 4

20g tamarind pulp
4 tbsp warm water
2 tbsp sugar
2 tbsp fish sauce
1 tsp finely chopped
   lemongrass
1 tbsp crushed garlic
1 tbsp gia vi (or a mix of
   2 parts sugar, 1 part
   sea salt, 1 part ground
   black pepper, 1 part
   garlic powder)
1 tsp chilli powder

Place the tamarind pulp in a small bowl, add just enough warm water to cover it, and soak for 10–20 minutes, until it becomes soft. Strain the juice into a mixing bowl.

Stir 2 tbsp of sugar into the tamarind juice. Gradually stir in the fish sauce and lemongrass, followed by the garlic, gia vi and the chilli powder. Depending on your palate, you may like the sauce slightly sourer, or sweeter, so adjust as you see fit.

COOK'S NOTES

Basic Ingredients

Eggs Whenever you can, buy free-range or organic eggs. They are more expensive but taste better. Buy them from the farmers' market where they are usually cheaper and fresher.

Gia vi This seasoning mix is especially popular in Northern Vietnamese cooking. It is a combination of garlic salt, sea salt, sugar and black pepper. The commercial type sold in oriental supermarkets will also contain a small amount of glutamate. To make your own, mix together 2 parts sugar, 1 part sea salt, 1 part ground black pepper and 1 part garlic powder and store in a jar.

Salt Use sea salt unless otherwise specified. Salt is used sparingly in Vietnamese cooking and is typically used for pickling or cleansing. Fish sauce is a more delicious alternative to flavour dishes.

Sugar Use caster sugar unless otherwise specified. Vietnamese cooking uses a variety of sugars, including palm sugar and rock sugar. However, we've found that caster sugar works just as well for most dishes.

Pepper Vietnam remains one of the main producers of pepper. Most is produced in the Central Highlands region, where the red basalt earth is ideal for growing it. The best pepper is said to come from the island of Phu Quoc. Use whole black peppercorns and grind them as you go to retain their intense flavour.

VIETNAMESE PANTRY (AND SUBSTITUTES)

Fresh Spices

Onions

We use the smaller red onions as we find they have more flavour and are easier to handle than large white onions.

Shallots

We are not fussed about using Thai or imported shallots from Asian countries. These usually have a deep red colour and a strong taste, but they are small and difficult to peel. Our favourites are banana shallots, usually of French origin. The round yellow shallots also work well.

Garlic

The easiest way to peel a garlic clove is to mash it first, using a mortar and pestle or the broad side of a knife, and then peel off the skin. We crush garlic in a food processor and then keep a small jar in the fridge for that week's cooking. Alternatively, you can chop the cloves as you go.

Ginger

Fresh ginger (ginger root) works well in broths and seafood dishes. English organic ginger is usually quite small. The most common fresh ginger is the large rhizome from China, and you can find it in greengrocers.

Galangal

Galangal looks similar to ginger, but its skin is smoother and it doesn't have ginger's lemony taste. We use galangal with fish and meat to make them fragrant. It's best to grind galangal using a pestle and mortar or a food processor. We buy it frozen from Asian supermarkets, thaw it in hot water and use as fresh.

Lemongrass

Lemongrass is one of the most versatile ingredients, and lends its aroma to any soup or grilled dish. We use both the whole fresh lemongrass stalks as well as chopped lemongrass, which you can find frozen in Asian supermarkets. Lemongrass can also be used to make tea.

Tamarind	The whole ripe fruit looks a bit like a broad bean, but is brown in colour. You can eat ripe tamarind, although typically it's used to add sourness to a dish. Tamarind is wonderful as it has a mild sourness and very fruity notes. Usually it's sold as a block of pulp in Asian supermarkets. We break a bit off from the block, then pour boiling hot water over it to dilute it and make tamarind juice (see p.73). We use tamarind juice in the same way as lemon or lime juice, in any recipe. *Note: if you can't find tamarind, use lemon or lime juice.*
Chillies	For a real spice kick, we use Scotch bonnets, green chillies from Kenya or red chillies from Thailand. They keep for months in the freezer, and we just take a couple out, wash them under the tap and they are like fresh.
Mushrooms	There are two types of mushrooms that are primarily used in Vietnamese cooking: shiitake and wood ear mushrooms. Shiitake, available fresh or dried, add flavour to meat and stocks. Wood ear mushrooms, available only in dried form, are usually mixed with meat to add crunch. We take a handful of dried mushrooms, pour hot water over them to rehydrate them and they can expand significantly. Wash the mushrooms carefully under running water before using as they may contain grains of sand. Squeeze out the water before slicing them.
Kaffir lime leaves	These come frozen and you can find them in Asian supermarkets. Wash a few leaves to thaw them and use a pair of scissors to cut them into thin strips. Sprinkle over chicken or white fish.

Fresh Herbs

Fresh herbs are one of the most prominent characteristics of Vietnamese cooking. Rarely is a meal served without a plateful of fresh herbs. Here we have listed the most popular and readily available herbs. To make your own herb plate, mix a few salad greens, round lettuce, a couple of slices of cucumber and any of the herbs opposite.

Many of these herbs can be found in large supermarkets, and Asian supermarkets have regular imports of the herbs into the UK. We find Turkish greengrocers offer the best value, as coriander, dill and mint are usually widely available and come in bigger bunches than you find in the supermarket.

Coriander

Coriander is perhaps the most versatile of herbs. We use the whole sprigs for garnishing just about any dish, and mix the chopped leaves with spring onion to use in soups. The large bunches look deceptively similar to parsley, but taste very different. Choose young coriander, as they are smaller and leafier, and without the hard stems, which we don't use anyway.

Mint

Spearmint, as you find it in greengrocers and supermarkets, is fine and keeps for a week or so in water. Use the leaves only.

Basil

Thai basil, as it is usually known, is different from the Italian basil, so don't use the latter as a substitute. Thai basil has green and pointy leaves and a quite unique aroma, reminiscent of cinnamon and cloves. It goes well with beef dishes.

Hot mint (Rau ram)

This herb is not easy to find but it's very rewarding when you do. Asian supermarkets often stock it. Herb growers in the UK also plant it and so you can sometimes find it in farmers' markets. Rau ram has a peppery taste that goes really well with meat and seafood.
Note: if you can't find rau ram, the closest substitute is coriander.

Shiso (Tia to)

You may have seen this herb on sushi plates in the UK but most people tend to discard them. The Vietnamese variety has both a deep red purple side and a green side. Shiso is said to have great healing qualities, and the Vietnamese equivalent of the Jewish chicken soup as a remedy for colds is a chicken rice soup with plenty of chopped tia to and spring onion.

Store Cupboard

Rice

In Vietnamese markets, you will find basketfuls of various types of rice, all freshly harvested. The Vietnamese typically use good-quality, long-grain jasmine rice. Personally, we prefer short-grain rice such as Korean arirang rice or sushi rice because they have the right degree of 'stickiness'. We don't use risotto rice, parboiled rice or basmati rice in Vietnamese dishes. Sometimes blending different types of rice can also work well. To cook rice you usually need 2 parts water to 1 part rice.

Rice paper

In Vietnam, rice paper is often made the traditional way from rice flour and water, which is formed into thin sheets, like crepes, and then sundried on large bamboo racks. The rice paper for export is usually factory-made and tends to be thicker, which makes it easier to handle, especially when making summer rolls. The most popular type is plain white with a diameter of 18–22cm. We recommend dabbing rice papers with warm water and then letting them rest on a wet cloth when preparing your rolls (see p.170–171), to prevent the papers from sticking and tearing.

Rice vermicelli noodles (Bun)

These are round, long noodles, a bit like spaghetti, but made with rice flour. They can be quite thick, about 1.2cm in diameter, which makes them suitable for noodle soups (such as *bun bo Hue*), or quite thin, 0.6cm in diameter, which makes them suitable for noodle salads. In Vietnam they are made fresh daily. But you can also get very good dried bun noodles (see p.209).

Flat rice noodles (Pho)

These flat noodles are used exclusively in *pho* dishes, either in noodle soups or stir-fries. They are quite similar to the Chinese ho fun noodles, although the Vietnamese version is thinner and has more elasticity. You can get fresh ho fun noodles from Chinese supermarkets or you can use the dehydrated type and rehydrate them in the same way as rice vermicelli noodles.

Cellophane or glass noodles (Mien)

These are very thin transparent noodles, made from mung beans or arrowroot. They can be quite brittle when dry and require gentle handling. As they get soft very quickly, they only need soaking in hot water before using, for instance in spring rolls. You can use glass noodles or rice vermicelli in many noodle soup recipes, so work with whatever you have to hand. As a general rule, glass noodles have their own flavour characteristics, whereas rice vermicelli noodles are neutral in flavour.

So for a clear broth like chicken, glass noodles work well. But for bold flavours, like the spicy *bun bo Hue*, or sweet and sour noodle soups, rice vermicelli noodles make a better starch base.

Dried shallots

Dried shallots are used liberally in Vietnamese salads, stir fries and noodle soups. You can buy them in jars from oriental supermarkets, or you can buy dried onion from any supermarket and lightly toast it. Alternatively, to make your own dried shallots, remove the skin from the shallots then slice into very thin rings and dehydrate by placing on a baking sheet in a cool oven (110°C/gas ¼) for an hour. Then fry them in hot oil in a frying pan until slightly brown, taking care not to burn them. Remove with a slotted spoon to a plate lined with a paper towel and let them rest. You can then use them immediately or store in the fridge for 2–3 weeks. If they turn soft in the fridge, revive them by placing in the oven at 180°C/gas 4 for a couple of minutes.

Roasted peanuts

Buy salted roasted peanuts and crush them coarsely in a food processor. Use to sprinkle on salads and vegetables or to make Peanut Sauce (see p.200).

Fermented Products

Fish sauce

Fish sauce is the holy grail of Vietnamese cuisine, and a good teaspoonful covers a multitude of sins. Traditionally it's made using only two ingredients, anchovies and salt. The fish are fermented in sea salt and kept in large wooden barrels in the shade for a year, after which the clear, golden liquid is extracted and bottled. The protein content of fish sauce is usually a good indicator of its quality, with the gourmet types containing around 42°N.

Shrimp paste

Fermented shrimp paste has a very pungent smell. However, diluting the shrimp paste (see opposite) for seasoning broths, or combining with garlic, lime juice and chilli, eliminates the pungent smell, leaving just the wonderful flavours.

Techniques

Meat carpaccio

Wrap the meat in clingfilm and place in the freezer for a couple of hours. The meat should be partly frozen, but not solid, when it comes out of the freezer. Use a sharp knife to cut thin slices of meat.

Fish carpaccio

For fish like sea bass, wrap in clingfilm and put in the freezer for 30 minutes before slicing thinly. Alternatively, cut thick slices of fish, wrap the individual slices in greaseproof paper and freeze for 20 minutes, then use a rolling pin to roll the fish until it flattens.

Making diluted shrimp paste

Pour cold water into a bowl, add the shrimp paste and stir well so the shrimp paste completely dissolves. Let this liquid rest for around 20 minutes. The liquid will stay at the top and the sediment will sit at the bottom. Pour the liquid into a separate bowl and discard the rest.

Cooking dried noodles

Noodles for the Vietnamese are like pasta for the Italians – they come in all shapes and sizes. Dried noodles taste as good as fresh ones if you use the correct technique. Remove the noodles from their packaging and put in a large bowl of cool water. Leave them to soak for 20 minutes. In a pan, bring to the boil enough water to cover the noodles and pour in a little oil to prevent them sticking. Add the drained noodles to the boiling water, turn down the heat and gently stir them. Cook until al dente (7–8 minutes for 400g). Once the noodles are tender, drain them, rinse under cool running water and untangle them with a fork.

STOCKISTS

Markets

Our first port of call for fresh, seasonal ingredients is always the farmers' market. In London, there is not only Broadway Market but a plethora of vibrant markets in most neighbourhoods with gorgeous produce. London Farmers Markets (www.lfm.org.uk) hold long-standing markets across London and we know of many other community-organised markets that have in recent years been conceived to serve local residents, such as Chatsworth Road E5, Venn Street SW4, Brockley Market SE4, and many more. The local authorities are also reviving many markets to better serve those living and working in the boroughs, such as Berwick Street Market WC1. Look out for when your local farmers' market is held.

We love the meat, fish and vegetables from our fellow stall holders, the likes of Ash Green Organics, Longwood Farm, Downland Produce, Coco&Me Cakes, and in every market you can find growers and farmers who are truly passionate about good food and pitch up in rain or shine. We probably do spend more at the markets than we could have at supermarkets, but the ingredients are better than restaurant-quality and with simple cooking, it's a beautiful way to eat better affordably.

Specialists

Ingredients such as fresh herbs, fish sauce and rice paper are now widely available in most supermarkets. We supplement by visiting the smaller Turkish/Indian/Bangladeshi/Jamaican grocers nearby for spices and ethnic produce, such as daikon (mooli) or tamarind. The following is a list of Vietnamese and oriental specialists, but, if you live in a major city, you can more than likely find what you need locally.

The London-based specialists listed offer a wider range of fresh products (e.g. fresh Vietnamese noodles for *pho*) as well as high-quality pantry ingredients (e.g. gourmet fish sauce and shrimp paste). Specialist shops like these can be found in many other major cities across the UK.

London Star Night
203–213 Mare St, Dalston, London E8 3QE

Long Dan
25 Hackney Rd, London E2 7NX

Duc Tien
Unit 2 Lombard Trading Estate, 51 Anchor & Hope Lane, SE7 7SN

See Woo
8–20 Lisle St, Chinatown, London
108 Horn Ln, Greenwich, London

Online Stores

Google makes it so easy to research and also buy ingredients, wherever you live. The online shopping section of many supermarkets has a full range of oriental ingredients. Additionally, the online specialists below also stock most of what you are likely to need.

Fusian
www.fusian.co.uk

See Woo
www.seewoo.com

Wing Yip
www.wingyip.com

Finally I want to reiterate that Vietnamese cooking and our ethos is all about versatility. So if you don't have access to authentic ingredients, use your imagination and improvise!

About the Authors

Van Tran and Anh Vu began their first market stall at Broadway Market in East London in 2009. Banhmi11 now has market stalls across London. They opened their first market café, No.101, in Shoreditch in 2012 and followed with No.17 in Clerkenwell in 2013.

Born in Vietnam, they both spent their childhoods in Hanoi, immersed in country's rich culinary traditions. Van and Anh received scholarships to come to the US and UK to study before meeting at Oxford University. They didn't train professionally as chefs but worked in finance in New York and London before leaving the City to pursue their passion.

Van and Anh have appeared on Jamie Oliver's *Great Britain* and Nigel Slater's *Simple Cooking*, and featured in the *Telegraph*, the *Guardian* and the *Observer*. Banhmi11 has been listed in the '100 Top Dishes in London', *Time Out* and 'The World's 10 Best Sandwiches', *ShortList* magazine.

They live in East London.

www.banhmi11.com

CRAFT YOUR OWN ...

BÁNH MÌ   £5
baguette fresh
toasted

BÚN   £6
Noodle salad with
rice vermicelli

CƠM   £6
Rice box with sushi
rice

All of our meals are served with
homemade pickles, market fresh greens,
pineapple sauce, dry shallot, peanuts.

Bánh : 11
Monday   11 - 4
Tuesday · Friday 11 - 18
Saturday   12 - 6

phát triển
đồng cỏ
chăn nuôi

Acknowledgements

Thanks to all our babies at Banhmi11, now and before. Thanks for believing in us and coming on board. You are and always will be our Banhmily.

Thanks to Ha Nguyen for holding down the fort. To Khanh, Thu Hoa, Hoa Pham, Thanh Ha, Thang, Trang, Trang Hoang, Hung, Tu Anh, Ngoc, Tu, Bao, Bao Anh, Quang Anh, Colin, Hong, Lucia, Phong, Aroune, Faizan, Waji and so many others for passing on the love.

Thanks to our families – we never see you enough, and we never say it in words, but we care. We owe you everything for who we are today.

Thanks to our friends, Boni, Lan Anh, chi Hien, anh Tuan, Judith, for keeping us sane.

Thanks to our ex-bosses, Staci and Bill, for your wisdom and training.

Thanks to our Broadway Market fellows, Tamami, Zita, Mike, Mathew, Dave, Jony. Thank you Andy Veitch for giving us the chance to get started.

Thanks to our architects and designers, Lirong, Patrick, Simon, for taking our dreams and making it a reality.

Thanks to our super-editor, Rowan Yapp for your patience and endless support. Thanks to Yuki, Valerie, Cynthia, Anna, Kim, for bringing the book to life. We have learned so much working with all of you.

But above all thanks to our customers for your support. You are the reason we are still here today. This is our chance to take food back to basics together – natural, beautiful and bountiful.

INDEX

Entries in *italics* indicate photographs.